NEW DIRECTIONS FOR CHILD DEVELOPM

William Damon, *Brown University*
EDITOR-IN-CHIEF

Promoting Community-Based Programs for Socialization and Learning

Francisco A. Villarruel
Michigan State University

Richard M. Lerner
Michigan State University

EDITORS

Number 63, Spring 1994

JOSSEY-BASS PUBLISHERS
San Francisco

PROMOTING COMMUNITY-BASED PROGRAMS FOR SOCIALIZATION AND LEARNING
Francisco A. Villarruel, Richard M. Lerner (eds.)
New Directions for Child Development, no. 63
William Damon, Editor-in-Chief

Microfilm copies of issues and articles are available in 16mm and 35mm, as well as microfiche in 105mm, through University Microfilms Inc., 300 North Zeeb Road, Ann Arbor, Michigan 48106-1346.

LC 85-644581   ISSN 0195-2269   ISBN 1-55542-721-9

NEW DIRECTIONS FOR CHILD DEVELOPMENT is part of The Jossey-Bass Education Series and is published quarterly by Jossey-Bass Inc., Publishers, 350 Sansome Street, San Francisco, California 94104-1342 (publication number USPS 494-090). Second-class postage paid at San Francisco, California, and at additional mailing offices. POSTMASTER: Send address changes to Jossey-Bass Inc., Publishers, 350 Sansome Street, San Francisco, California 94104-1342.

EDITORIAL CORRESPONDENCE should be sent to the Editor-in-Chief, William Damon, Department of Education, Box 1938, Brown University, Providence, Rhode Island 02912.

Cover photograph by Wernher Krutein/PHOTOVAULT © 1990.

Manufactured in the United States of America. Nearly all Jossey-Bass books, jackets, and periodicals are printed on recycled paper that contains at least 50 percent recycled waste, including 10 percent postconsumer waste. Many of our materials are also printed with vegetable-based inks; during the printing process, these inks emit fewer volatile organic compounds (VOCs) than petroleum-based inks. VOCs contribute to the formation of smog.

CONTENTS

EDITORS' NOTES

The developmental contextual view of a child's learning processes posits that children learn and become socialized in relation to the characteristics of specific environments. From this perspective, learning cannot be explained by reference to processes that exist at one level of organization, for example, the child or his or her environment. Rather, like any other human characteristic or functional process, learning must be explained through analysis of relations between each child and the multiple contexts within which he or she functions. Over time, the multiple contexts in which a child functions may work together as an interactive force that supplements, enhances, or diminishes a child's learning performance and abilities. Accordingly, a child's learning both in school and after school must be appraised before the totality of that child's learning can be identified. In addition, learners' multicontextual developmental relations must be the target of not only developmental description and explanation but, critically, interventions as well. U.S. society is at a point in its history where interventions in children's multicontextual developmental relations are imperative because these relations often reflect societal problems that affect childhood learning. Intervention programs are also needed because, both in school and after school, behaviors are being socialized and, indeed, institutionalized that place the children who acquire these behaviors at risk of having severely diminished chances for healthy lives. When children are at risk, the society they will grow up to inhabit is also at risk.

Over the last decade, several researchers have noted that not only are youths engaging in an increasing number of antisocial and self-defeating behaviors, but they are doing so at earlier ages (Dryfoos, 1990; Hamburg, 1992). In response to these changing behaviors and other societal changes (for instance, the structure of the American family [Hernandez, 1993]), naturally occurring social networks in the community and safe environments within which youth can gather have gradually diminished. In reaction to both of these distressing trends, youth-serving professionals, and adolescents themselves, have begun to develop innovative programs that provide alternative choices for youths. Most noteworthy among these efforts are programs that are contextually responsive to the needs and issues of youths and their families and the communities in which they reside. These programs provide environments that promote positive opportunities for children's socialization and learning.

The chapters in this volume describe and analyze five distinct types of programs that seek to promote knowledge, competence, and a sense of belonging for diverse youths. As these programs illustrate, community-based youth development programs that provide children and adolescents with opportunities for healthy development and safe environments in which to interact with and learn from their peers also offer opportunities for these youths to learn and practice social skills and to apply and consolidate academic abilities and interests. The programs presented in this volume underscore the idea that programs that are innovative in linking children's and adolescents' development to community contexts can effectively address the risks that beset so many children in the United States today.

This volume exists due to the effort and commitment of the chapter authors and of the series editor-in-chief, William Damon. Their belief in the importance of the work discussed in this volume and the collegial cooperation they demonstrated were the vital ingredients enabling our editorial work to proceed productively.

Finally, the authors of this volume wish to express their gratitude to Peter Gerber of the John D. and Catherine T. MacArthur Foundation. The work of the editors was supported in part by a grant from the W. K. Kellogg Foundation. We are grateful to the foundation for its assistance.

Francisco A. Villarruel
Richard M. Lerner
Editors

References

Dryfoos, J. G. *Adolescents at Risk: Prevalence and Prevention.* New York: Oxford University Press, 1990.

Hamburg, D. A. *Today's Children: Creating a Future for a Generation in Crisis.* New York: Time Books, 1992.

Hernandez, D. J. *America's Children: Resources from Family, Government, and the Economy.* New York: Russell Sage Foundation, 1993.

FRANCISCO A. VILLARRUEL *is assistant professor in the Department of Family and Child Ecology and at the Institute for Children, Youth, and Families and a research associate with the Julian Samora Research Institute at Michigan State University.*

RICHARD M. LERNER *is professor of family and child ecology; psychology; pediatrics and human development; and counseling, educational psychology, and special education, as well as director of the Institute for Children, Youth, and Families, Michigan State University.*

Developmental contextualism provides a theoretical frame for the
design of after-school programs for children and youths.

Development and Context
and the Contexts of Learning

Francisco A. Villarruel, Richard M. Lerner

The processes by which humans develop have been explained from diverse metatheoretical and theoretical perspectives (Lerner, 1986; Overton, 1984; Reese and Overton, 1970). Traditionally, these perspectives have stressed that the key bases of development lie within the individual *or* in the environment surrounding him or her *or* in the interaction between the individual and the environment (Lerner, 1986). Over the past two decades, there has been increasing theoretical and empirical interest among scientists studying human development in the latter, interactive notions of development (Baltes, 1987; Lerner, 1978, 1986, 1991; Overton, 1973, 1984), and this interest has now evolved into a refined understanding of the role of the context, or ecology, of human development (Bronfenbrenner, 1977, 1979; Bronfenbrenner and Crouter, 1983) and the role of the systemic interdependence among changes associated with the individual and changes associated with his or her complex ecology (Ford and Lerner, 1992). In particular, the theory of *developmental contextualism* (Lerner, 1991, 1992; Lerner and Kauffman, 1985) is a useful frame for discussing the dynamic linkages between the development of a child's individual characteristics (for example, cognitive abilities) and the diverse and changing ecology within which the child lives.

From the developmental contextual perspective, the basic process of human development involves the changing *relations* between the person and the multiple levels of his or her physical and social ecology, or context (Lerner, 1991, 1992). That is, the biological and psychological characteristics of the

The writing of this chapter was supported in part by a grant from the W. K. Kellogg Foundation.

developing individual and the characteristics of his or her familial, neighborhood, community, societal, and cultural contexts change interdependently, or are fused (Tobach and Greenberg, 1984), across that individual's life span. This person-context fusion means that explanations of *any* behavioral or developmental characteristic or process require both a relational and a developmental perspective. For instance, emotional or cognitive processes do not unfold independently of context; rather, they are products of the linkages between a specific person and specific contexts (Baltes, 1987; Featherman, 1983; Lerner, 1984). In addition, because individuals' contexts have a historical, or temporal, component, all person-context processes have a temporal component. Accordingly, in order to account for the specific characteristics of an individual's emotional or cognitive functioning or personality, one must again pursue a developmental analysis, that is, a systematic temporal analysis (Ford and Lerner, 1992), *and* a multicontextual analysis, and treat these two parameters of inquiry in relational terms. Moreover, in attempts either to fully describe behavior or to design adequate intervention programs, identical parameters must be used. If, for example, a child's cognitive characteristics exist relationally, then the multiple contexts within which that child lives need to be appraised in order to describe a particular cognitive characteristic (for example, reading ability, cognitive style, or linguistic skill) without confounding it with a particular setting (for example, the classroom) within which that characteristic has been observed. Also, multiple occasions of observation must underlie descriptions in order to disentangle unitemporal patterns of covariation from change trajectories.

Similarly, when youth-serving professionals design interventions, the efforts must extend to the multiple settings within which the child lives (for example, the home, the school, the peer group), that is, the areas of the community within which the child interacts when not in school (Dryfoos, 1990). If developmental change is ubiquitous and if multicontextual interventions are required, they must be extended over time, simply because a one-time "inoculation" will not suffice to alter the course of an individual's development across his or her entire life span (Baltes, 1987; Lerner, 1984; Lerner and Ryff, 1978) when the person-context relationship remains open to change (Ford and Lerner, 1992; Lerner, 1984; Steele, Miller, and Rai, 1993).

Contexts for Learning

The developmental contextual perspective has important implications for understanding a child's learning processes. Clearly, within this perspective, human learning is not explainable by analysis of single variables or processes (an individual's genetic makeup for example). Like all other human functioning, learning must be analyzed in terms of the relationships between the child and the multiple contexts within which he or she functions and not merely assessed within any one setting, such as schools (Carnegie Council on Adolescent Development, 1992; Children's Defense Fund, 1992; Comer, 1990).

Learning both inside and outside school must be appraised, and because the child is a continuous element across his or her contextual domains, relations across as well as within contexts are an important feature of the analysis of learning (compare Bronfenbrenner, 1977, 1979).

Moreover, because a child's development is incessant even as key features of his or her contexts change continuously over time, not only must a child's learning characteristics be appraised inside and outside the school setting, but both these contextual domains must be assessed longitudinally in order to understand a child's learning. Such changes can occur within settings, as changes in the structure and function of the peer group do across childhood (Norris and Rubin, 1984), or different contexts can emerge or become salient at different times in a child's life. For example, the part-time workplace emerges as a key setting for adolescents who are full-time high school students (Steinberg, 1983).

Simply, then, contexts for learning exist wherever children spend their time. And over time, these contexts may enter into relationships that add to or diminish a child's learning performance and abilities. Thus, youth-serving professionals seeking to develop effective learning programs should focus their developmental explanations and observations and especially their interventions in terms of learner-multicontext relations. As we described in our editors' notes to this volume, multicontextual, relational, and developmental interventions are imperative at this time in U.S. society not only because of issues directly related to childhood learning. Once it is apparent that relations between contexts and development do shape children's characteristics, it is also apparent that the characteristics being developed by children in the diverse settings within which they spend their days involve behaviors that extend far beyond those associated with the traditional academic content. In school and after school, children are acquiring behaviors that are severely reducing their opportunities for living lives that both the children and the society will find fulfilling.

Features of Contemporary Youth Socialization

Fundamental changes in U.S. family life, communities, and society as a whole, and in particular the well-documented problems of the U.S. educational system (Carnegie Council on Adolescent Development, 1989; Edward and Young, 1992), have contributed to the perception that this is a nation at risk, one with a generation of children and adolescents who have severely constrained life chances (Dryfoos, 1990; Hamburg, 1992; Schorr, 1988). A central question about the societal changes that have occurred in this nation is whether the opportunity now exists for most adolescents to experience positive and healthy opportunities for growth, development, and socialization. The question arises as a consequence of increases in the percentage of children living in single-parent families, increases in the prevalence of child and youth poverty, and decreases in opportunities for the young adolescents who live under conditions of persistent and pervasive poverty to interact positively with adults and peers (Center for the Study of Social Policy, 1993).

Adolescents are not only exhibiting more antisocial and self-defeating behaviors than they did just a decade ago, they are doing so at earlier ages (Keith and Nelson, 1990). The higher rates of teen pregnancy, substance abuse and misuse, depression, violence and suicide, and school failure and under-achievement—in addition to higher rates of poor health, inadequate nutrition, and neglect and abuse—are not only minimizing adolescents' chances for healthy lives but are also negatively affecting community and individual well-being (Benson, 1993; Dryfoos, 1990; Fuchs and Reklis, 1992; Hamburg, 1992; National Council of Administrators of Home Economics Programs, 1991; Scales, 1991; Simons, Finlay, and Yang, 1991). Furthermore, as a reaction to the changes mentioned here and other societal changes, naturally occurring social networks in the community (Bernard, 1991) and safe environments where adolescents can gather are growing fewer. The 1988 National Educa-tional Longitudinal Study, for example, which surveyed a nationally represen-tative sample of about 25,000 eighth graders, found that approximately 27 percent of the respondents regularly spent two or more hours home alone after school. Moreover, eighth graders from families in the lowest socioeconomic groups were more likely to report that they were home alone for more than three hours, while those in the highest income groups were least likely to be unsupervised for that amount of time (Benson, 1993; U.S. Department of Edu-cation, Office of Educational Research and Improvement and National Center for Education Statistics, 1990). Yet, as recently reported by the Carnegie Coun-cil on Adolescent Development (1992), young adolescents do not want to be left alone or left to their own devices. Rather, they want more regular contact with adults who care about and respect them; they want more opportunities to contribute to their communities; they desire protection from the hazards of drugs, violence, and gangs; and they seek greater access to constructive and attractive alternatives to loneliness (Benson, 1993).

Responses to Problems of Youth Socialization

In reaction to the distressing trends among youths and to recent reports that have detailed the difficult issues confronting adolescents (Carnegie Council on Adolescent Development, 1992; Center for the Study of Social Policy, 1993; Keith and others, 1993; W. T. Grant Foundation, 1988), communities, youth-serving professionals, and adolescents themselves have begun to develop inno-vative programs that provide alternative choices for youths. Most noteworthy among these efforts are programs that are contextually responsive to the needs and issues of youths, their families, and the communities in which they reside. These programs provide environments that allow youths to experience posi-tive opportunities for socialization and learning. The importance of these pro-grams and their informal learning environments is twofold. First, they promote responsive communities, which in turn help build strong families in the inter-est of youths (Keith and others, 1993; W. T. Grant Foundation, 1988). Second, they provide safe settings where children can gather with peers and adults (Heath and McLaughlin, 1993).

Each of the five remaining chapters in this volume discusses particular groups or programs that try to provide knowledge, competence, and a sense of belonging for diverse youths. In Chapter Two, Laura Martin and Carol Ascher illustrate how the Children's Television Workshop designs mathematics and science video materials that are used in children's informal education in before- and after-school programs. A key focus in successful program design, they argue, is that the activities and materials can be readily adapted to the contexts in which they are used.

In Chapter Three, Shirley Brice Heath describes the results of a five-year study of youth organizations located in the inner cities of three major U.S. metropolitan communities. She reports that the organizations youths regarded as effective were the ones that provided them with choices of activities and groups that they wanted to join. Moreover, Heath notes that youths preferred authentic assessment (that is, performance-related assessment) of programs. Programs whose evaluations included group-endorsed projects requiring practice and summative performances, such as dance recitals, Little League baseball games, and drama and dance teams formed to "perfect" performances prior to public performances, were the ones that provided youths with the skills to interact effectively both inside and outside the youth organizations. Thus, Heath and other researchers have found that today's youths tend to be attracted to, and maintain their participation in, programs in which they can be active and social and can assume central leadership roles in the planning and structuring of activities (Heath and McLaughlin, 1993; Steele, Miller, and Rai, 1993).

In Chapter Four, Miriam Schustack and her colleagues discuss the cognitive and social developments that occur among school-age children enrolled in a multisite, community-based, computer-oriented after-school activity. The authors of this chapter observe that, in addition to the development of bilingual and computer literacy skills, other academic skills are enhanced and shared knowledge is generated as a consequence of interactions among this activity's participants, volunteers, and instructors.

The centrality of youths' participation to program effectiveness is also emphasized by Thomas Hatch and his colleagues in their description of a self-directed, project-based after-school learning program in Chapter Five. Key program elements that they identify include the establishment of common expectations among participants, program volunteers, and instructors; identification and resolution of practical constraints (regarding funding and other resources for example); evolution of program content to meet the goals of the participants; and development of procedures to enable participants to create their own projects.

Among the various contexts with which any successful youth program must interrelate, the family is key (Dryfoos, 1990; Schorr, 1988). In Chapter Six, Catherine Cooper and her colleagues report their findings that parental aspirations for a child's future and the links between the family and the resources of the community vary in relation to whether the family is of Mexican American or European American background; variation occurs also in relation to the child's age.

Conclusion

All the chapters in this volume illustrate that both theory and empirical evidence strongly support the idea that community-based programs are essential to the healthy development of young adolescents. An underlying assumption of such programs is that youths will develop positively as a result of their contact with a variety of safe and authentic experiences, caring persons, and supportive systems. The programs described in this volume support this assumption.

As evidenced by the chapters in this volume, community-based youth development programs that offer healthy development and safe settings for children and adolescents and encourage positive peer interaction and learning require the implementation of four objectives: the promotion of social competence; the development of problem-solving skills; the creation of a sense of autonomy, which allows individuals to develop their identity and ability to act independently and to have an opportunity to exert control over their environment; and the instillation of a sense of purpose and an orientation toward the future. Moreover, such programs endeavor to provide children and adolescents with community supports that link to both the family and the school, and thus endow these youths with a wider view of issues, events, and people than they have previously had. These community programs offer opportunities for youths to acquire and gain experience in using social skills and to put their academic abilities and interests to use in new or different ways and to integrate separately acquired abilities and interests. The programs also provide a forum for youths to discuss how adult roles involve caring for others, and they offer youths chances to test a variety of potential work roles, to seek (and supply) support across generations, and to develop a sense of competence and responsibility.

In sum, the contributions to this volume substantiate previous theory and research that suggest the value of community-based programs in facilitating the health and well-being of children and adolescents. The programs discussed contain rich examples of efforts that meet children's and adolescents' needs by providing supportive environments that are developmentally and contextually sensitive and that promote engagement in a variety of active socializing experiences. These programs underscore the idea that innovative approaches that link the development of youths to community contexts can effectively address the issues of risk that beset so many of today's children and adolescents in the United States (Bernard, 1991; Clark, 1988).

References

Baltes, P. B. "Theoretical Propositions of Life-Span Developmental Psychology: On the Dynamics Between Growth and Decline." *Developmental Psychology*, 1987, 23, 611–626.

Benson, P. L. *The Troubled Journey: A Portrait of 6th–12th Grade Youth*. Minneapolis, Minn.: Search Institute, 1993.

Bernard, B. *Fostering Resiliency and Kids: Protective Factors in the Family, School, and Community*. Portland, Oreg.: Northwest Regional Educational Laboratories, Western Regional Center for Drug-free School and Communities, 1991.

Bronfenbrenner, U. "Toward an Experimental Ecology of Human Development." *American Psychologist*, 1977, *32*, 513–531.

Bronfenbrenner, U. *The Ecology of Human Development*. Cambridge, Mass.: Harvard University Press, 1979.

Bronfenbrenner, U., and Crouter, A. C. "The Evolution of Environmental Models in Developmental Research." In W. Kersen (ed.), *Handbook of Child Psychology*. Vol 1: *History, Theories, and Methods*. New York: Wiley, 1983.

Carnegie Council on Adolescent Development. *Turning Points: Preparing American Youth for the 21st Century*. New York: Carnegie Corporation, 1989.

Carnegie Council on Adolescent Development. *A Matter of Time: Risk and Opportunity in the Nonschool Hours*. New York: Carnegie Corporation of New York, 1992.

Center for the Study of Social Policy. *Kids Count Data Book*. Washington, D.C.: Center for the Study of Social Policy, 1993.

Children's Defense Fund. *Child Poverty up Nationally and in 33 States*. Washington, D.C.: Children's Defense Fund, 1992.

Clark, R. M. *Critical Factors in Why Disadvantaged Students Succeed or Fail in School*. New York: Academy for Educational Development, 1988.

Comer, J. P. "Home, School, and Academic Learning." In J. I. Goodlad and P. Keating (eds.), *Access to Knowledge: An Agenda for Our Nation's Schools*. New York: College Entrance Examination Board, 1990.

Dryfoos, J. G. *Adolescents at Risk: Prevalence and Prevention*. New York: Oxford University Press, 1990.

Edward, P. A., and Young, L. "Beyond Parents: Family, Community, and School Involvement." *Phi Delta Kappan*, 1992, *74*, 72–80.

Featherman, D. L. "Life-Span Perspectives in Social Science Research." In P. B. Baltes and O. G. Brim, Jr. (eds.), *Life-Span Development and Behavior*. Vol. 5. San Diego, Calif.: Academic Press, 1983.

Ford, D. L., and Lerner, R. M. *Developmental Systems Theory: An Integrative Approach*. Newbury Park, Calif.: Sage, 1992.

Fuchs, V. R., and Reklis, D. M. "America's Children: Economic Perspectives and Policy Options." *Science*, 1992, *25*, 41–46.

Hamburg, D. A. *Today's Children: Creating a Future for a Generation in Crisis*. New York: Time Books, 1992.

Heath, S. B., and McLaughlin, M. W. *Identity and Inner-City Youth: Beyond Ethnicity and Gender*. New York: Teachers College Press, 1993.

Keith, J. G., and Nelson, C. *Michigan Early Adolescence Survey II*. East Lansing: Michigan State University, 1990.

Keith, J. G., Perkins, D. F., Zhou, Z., Clifford, M. C., Gilmore, B., and Townsend, M. Z. *Building and Maintaining Community Coalitions on Behalf of Children, Youth, and Families*. Report no. 529. East Lansing: Michigan State University, Agricultural Experiment Station, 1993.

Lerner, R. M. "Nature, Nurture, and Dynamic Interactionism." *Human Development*, 1978, *21*, 1–20.

Lerner, R. M. *On the Nature of Human Plasticity*. New York: Cambridge University Press, 1984.

Lerner, R. M. *Concepts and Theories of Human Development*. (2nd ed.) New York: Random House, 1986.

Lerner, R. M. "Changing Organism-Context Relations as the Basic Process of Development: A Developmental Contextual Perspective." *Developmental Psychology*, 1991, *27*, 27–32.

Lerner, R. M. *Final Solutions: Biology, Prejudice, and Genocide*. University Park: Pennsylvania State University, 1992.

Lerner, R. M., and Kauffman, M. B. "The Concept of Development in Contextualism." *Developmental Review*, 1985, *5*, 309–333.

Lerner, R. M., and Ryff, C. D. "Implementation of the Life-Span View of Human Development: The Sample Case of Attachment." In P. B. Baltes (ed.), *Life-Span Development and Behavior*. Vol. 1. San Diego, Calif.: Academic Press, 1978.

National Council of Administrators of Home Economics Programs. *Creating a Vision: The Profession for the Next Century*. Report of the working conference, Oct. 1991. Pine Mountain, Ga.: Callaway Gardens, 1991.

Norris, J., and Rubin, K. H. "Social Interaction and Communication: A Life-Span Perspective." In P. B. Baltes and O. G. Brim., Jr. (eds.), *Life-Span Development and Behavior*. Vol. 6. San Diego, Calif.: Academic Press, 1984.

Overton, W. F. "On the Assumptive Base of the Nature-Nurture Controversy: Additive Versus Interactive Conceptions." *Human Development*, 1973, *16*, 74–89.

Overton, W. F. "World Views and Their Influence on Psychological Theory and Research: Kuhn-Kakatos-Lauden." In H. W. Reese (ed.), *Advances in Child Development and Behavior*. Vol. 18. San Diego, Calif.: Academic Press, 1984.

Reese, H. W., and Overton, W. F. "Models of Development and Theories of Development." In L. R. Goulet and P. B. Baltes (eds.), *Life-Span Developmental Psychology: Research and Theory*. San Diego, Calif.: Academic Press, 1970.

Scales, P. C. *A Portrait of Young Adolescents in the 1990s: Implications for Promoting Health, Growth, and Development*. Carrboro, N.C.: Center for Early Adolescence, 1991.

Schorr, L. B. *Within Our Reach: Breaking the Cycle of Disadvantage*. New York: Doubleday, 1988.

Simons, J. M., Finlay, B., and Yang, A. *The Adolescent and Young Adult Fact Book*. Washington, D.C.: Children's Defense Fund, 1991.

Steele, S. M., Miller, T. F., and Rai, K. *Nationwide Participation in 4-H During the 1980's: Information from the Office of Education NELS:88 Study*. Madison: University of Wisconsin, Madison Cooperative Extension, 1993.

Steinberg, L. "The Varieties and Effects of Work During Adolescence." In M. Lamb, A. Brown, and B. Rogoff (eds.), *Advances in Developmental Psychology*. Vol. 3. Hillsdale, N.J.: Erlbaum, 1983.

Tobach, E., and Greenberg, G. "The Significance of T. C. Schneirla's Contribution to the Concept of Levels of Integration." In G. Greenberg and E. Tobach (eds.), *Behavioral Evolution and Integrative Levels*. Hillsdale, N.J.: Erlbaum, 1984.

U.S. Department of Education, Office of Educational Research and Improvement and National Center for Education Statistics. *National Educational Longitudinal Study of 1988: A Profile of the American Eighth Grader*. Washington, D.C.: U.S. Government Printing Office, 1990.

W. T. Grant Foundation. *The Forgotten Half: Pathways to Success for America's Youth and Young Families*. Washington, D.C.: Youth and America's Future, the W. T. Grant Commission on Work, Family, and Citizenship, 1988.

FRANCISCO A. VILLARRUEL *is assistant professor in the Department of Family and Child Ecology and at the Institute for Children, Youth, and Families and a research associate with the Julian Samora Research Institute at Michigan State University.*

RICHARD M. LERNER *is professor of family and child ecology; psychology; pediatrics and human development; and counseling, educational psychology, and special education, as well as director of the Institute for Children, Youth, and Families, Michigan State University.*

This chapter presents the model of research content development and production processes used by the Children's Television Workshop for math and science materials for school age child care programs.

Developing Math and Science Materials for School Age Child Care Programs

Laura Martin, Carol Ascher

Over the last three years, the Children's Television Workshop (CTW) has been developing materials for children's after-school programs. Because CTW relies very heavily on research in producing its materials, their development provides a unique opportunity for investigating both the current state of after-school care and the possibilities confronting designers of materials for these settings. The CTW Model (see Figure 2.1) shows how research, content development, and production processes are integrated as materials are developed.

It was particularly important that we follow the model in the development of after-school materials because of our general unfamiliarity with the needs of people in these settings. So, to learn about the needs of after-school programs for developing the materials, the CTW research department reviewed the relevant literature, conducted twelve separate studies in centers across the country, and talked with many program and curriculum experts in the field. In all, this research involved approximately six hundred group leaders in fourteen cities and several hundred children. Brief descriptions of the studies may be found in the appendix to this chapter. Most of the research was conducted in centers located in poor or working class neighborhoods, much among ethnic minority children. The research included a variety of programs, among them ones run by national organizations such as the YMCA and Boys and Girls

The observational studies discussed here were conducted by Inverness Research Associates: Mark St. John, Barbara Heenan, Teri Pavia, Deborah Perry, Felisa Tibbets, Becky McClaskey. Thanks also to Barbara Myerson Katz and Hezel Associates for their contributions to our research.

Figure 2.1. Children's Television Workshop Research, Development, and Production Model

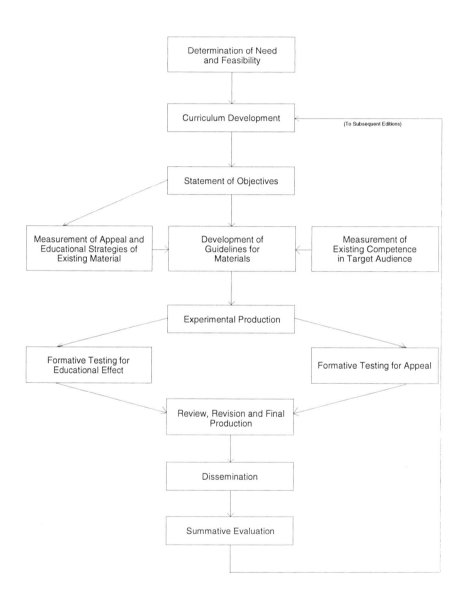

Source: Adapted from presentation materials of the International Television Group, Children's Television Workshop.

Clubs. Finally, CTW invited a group of seven after-school program and curriculum specialists to discuss current issues in after-school care. This chapter reviews what we learned about both the programs and the design and use of educational materials in after-school settings.

Background

An estimated 13 million U.S. children under the age of twelve have parents who work and cannot be home when their children start out for or get out of school (Rogan and Graves, 1989). Increasingly, these children, especially in the five- to twelve-year-old age group, have begun to participate in what are called school age child care programs (SACCs). Most often, children attend between 2:30 p.m. and 6:00 to 6:30 p.m., with some also participating in before-school care. About 84 percent of the children attend daily, for an average of three hours per afternoon. Owing to scheduling differences, however, a program's full group of students may only remain together for around ninety minutes (Katz, 1990a).

School age child care programs across the country are relatively new: about half of all SACCs have been in existence for under five years. These SACC programs are run under a variety of auspices, including the local public school systems, private schools, churches, city parks and recreation departments, youth-serving organizations such as the YMCA, and community agencies. At present, there are no national regulations for SACCs. Staff member-to-child ratios vary from 1:1 to 1:25 (Marx, 1990). SACC staff varies in training and certification. For example, a CTW survey of 130 centers in six cities found that 40 percent of the staff were full-time and 38 percent part-time, with licensed teachers representing 20 percent and volunteers a mere 3 percent (Katz, 1990a). Much like preschool professionals, most SACC staff throughout the country work at the bottom of the pay scale. Program resources vary widely, with some programs spending as much as $3,000 yearly on materials and some having no materials budget at all. The majority spend between $0 and $250 on materials (Martin and Shapiro, 1990).

Briefly, all the centers share the goals of keeping the children safe, of creating positive environments for children's social growth, and of providing engaging activities for children. Most offer predominantly recreational activities, with occasional emphasis on academic tutoring or enrichment and clubs. Weekly trips, community service (for example, participating in clean-up campaigns) and occasional movies, television, and videos are also provided. Most centers appear to offer small- and large-group activities, as well as opportunities for a child to be alone (Dyrud, 1989). The majority offer arts and crafts to occupy them. A survey conducted in Alabama, Georgia, Tennessee, and Mississippi (Rogan and Graves, 1989) provides a sample of activity distribution in centers. In this study over three-quarters provided homework assistance, planned recreation, and snacks; around two-thirds offered access to a school library, arts and crafts, and tutoring. It is interesting that only one-third provided opportunities like field trips, computer use, or other special enrichment.

One constraint on activities in these centers is the amount of time leaders spend in planning them. Surveys as well as site visits conducted by CTW found that most leaders spend less than half an hour, on average, planning for a given activity (Inverness Research Associates, 1991; Maguire Associates, 1991; Martin and Shapiro, 1990).

Although one Children's Television Workshop survey suggests that centers want their programming to become more educational in the next five years, administrators and group leaders emphasized that "such goals are frequently unrealistic in after-school programs where children come in tired from a full day of school, wanting to relax" (Katz, 1990a, p. 8). It may also be unrealistic given the training of staff, the staff-to-student ratio, the amount of money available for resources, and the amount of staff time spent planning.

Theories of Appropriate After-School Programming

Given the limits of current after-school child care facilities, it is useful to compare expert views of appropriate after-school programming to the reality. This programming represents a potpourri of recreation, school, and agency philosophies. Researchers, administrators, and curriculum specialists use terms like *decompress, noncompetitive, peer control, teacher-facilitated, child-centered, choice and flexibility*, and *not school reinforcement* to describe the qualities they believe should characterize SACCs (Martin, 1990; School-Age Child Care Council, 1989; New York State Council on Children and Families, 1988). They warn against too much structure, which is said to cause children to lose touch with the personal creativity through which they work out emotional conflicts and develop intellectually (Armstrong, 1990). The School-Age Child Care Council (1989, p. 1) argues that "an enrichment philosophy is the most developmentally appropriate for meeting the needs of school-age children during nonschool hours." In the same vein, the New York State Council on Children and Families (1988) recommends that program activities capitalize on the centers' special subcultures, providing "ample opportunities for children to form their own groups or clubs" and allowing children to plan and develop their own projects, such as plays or newsletters. The council argues that homework should not be required or become the focus of the program, and that school experiences should not be repeated in the hours before or after school, although school experiences can be supplemented or complemented during this time.

The professional views of what children need seem utopian given the straits in which school age child care centers currently operate. However, work can certainly be done to promote some of this philosophy in the SACC setting. One such attempt is represented by the current effort of the Children's Television Workshop to provide stimulating, affordable materials for SACC programs.

CTW Materials

Realizing that many low-achieving children increasingly spend significant portions of their free time in institutional settings, CTW has developed projects that seek to extend children's informal education in school age child care settings. These projects involve videos, activity cards, games, and puzzles that are based on CTW video productions. One kit of materials is based on the science show "3-2-1 Contact"; another is based on the math show "Square One TV." Both these kits include an instructional video and printed materials for group leaders in addition to the videos and hands-on activities for children.

Three studies, completed in the spring of 1990, looked at how SACC staff used these science and math kits in actual after-school programs (Inverness Research Associates, 1991; Hezel Associates, 1991; Katz, 1991). CTW researchers designed the studies and then collaborated with independent research groups to carry them out. Two of the studies, lasting three months each, looked at forty-seven centers in two cities and employed broad-based survey, interview, and log techniques. The third study consisted of intensive observations and interviews over six weeks in six sites in three cities. The results told us how group leaders interpreted the math and science activities and integrated them into different types of programs. They also told us how materials designers could improve their offerings given the limits of current child care settings. Through these studies, we identified several issues as critical in the design of successful materials: the fit of the materials into the variety of social and educational goals, time frames and schedules of after-school programs, and constraints on staff, space, attendance, and resources.

A Glimpse at the Programs

To make the results of our investigations more vivid for the reader, we start by describing three of the six centers in which the observational study took place. The descriptions are excerpted from researchers' field notes and give some sense of the differences in program settings and approaches.

Settlement House Program. This center serves economically disadvantaged and minority groups in a large Midwestern city. The settlement house in which it is located offers a variety of services, such as Headstart, homeless drop-in, and senior citizens programs. These meet in an old school building, which is open nights and weekends. The forty-five children in the after-school program are divided into three age groupings (five to seven, six to nine, and eight to twelve years old), each of which has a group worker in charge. There are four staff members all together, and all have completed or almost completed their bachelor's degree and have varying experience in fields concerned with early childhood. Children attend the after-school program for one to three hours daily during the school year.

The program follows a High Scope curriculum and is described as "kid initiated, teacher facilitated." It is also a place to keep kids safe. It was described as "not a school" but a child care center for working families that helps children improve their social and emotional skills. It seeks to help children express and enrich themselves and improve their self-esteem.

The after-school program is well supplied, with plenty of the staples but also with special materials like yarn, paper plates, and scrounged materials. A videocassette recorder and television are available on another floor in a Headstart room. At circle time, the children choose from a number of planned and unplanned activities, including arts and crafts, reading stories, playing house, using blocks, and playing games. Free choice is an important component of the program.

The CTW math and science kits appeared to fit in well with the planned/free-choice program format. They appeared to function best as an additional activity option. By the end of the study, the math materials were being used almost exclusively by the older group, while the science cards served as catalysts for younger children's activity. Because the VCR was on another floor, video viewing violated the free-choice nature of the environment, and so was of less interest than the activities themselves, which can be used in a stand-alone manner.

School-Based Remedial Math Program. This after-school program was a temporary one, running in a classroom in a Northeastern inner-city elementary school. Most of the students were black or Hispanic, the majority getting free or reduced-price lunches. It met twice a week for about an hour over several months. Fourteen students, latchkey children, were chosen to participate; eight children, mostly boys, attended regularly. Conceived of and operated by a fifth grade teacher with fourteen years' teaching experience, the program was designed to help students improve their basic math skills and to keep students in a safe environment a few extra hours a week. It was also one part of the school's efforts to help lower dropout rates and to reach out into the community. A small but active parent group organizes workshops and about a half dozen other after-school classes. This program was funded by a small grant.

The specific goal of the teacher, in addition to reinforcing skills, was to build children's self-esteem and comfort with math. Prior to the introduction of the math kit, the teacher offered the children Cuisenaire rods, manipulatives, and recycled materials to use. When the math kit was used, the teacher showed a videotape at each session while she set up several math games from which the children could choose. She also set up an arts and crafts alternative, which was never chosen. The teacher worked as a facilitator for the math activities, but she also began to use access to the games as leverage to get the kids to quiet down, finish their homework, cooperate, and so forth. The level of children's engagement with the materials, nonetheless, was consistently high.

YMCA Program. This program serves children K–6 four or five hours a day during the school year. It meets in a portable classroom on the site of an elementary school near the U.S.-Mexican border. The fifty-five children are from Hispanic, white, Filipino, and black middle-income families. Two leaders and two aides as well as a site supervisor are on site. The leaders have training and experience in child care. All have high school diplomas. Leaders at this site had received training by the YMCA on the use of the kits.

The program was originally a school-sponsored one called Project Safe. Recently, the YMCA had taken over sponsorship, which meant a cut in pay for staff as well as new regulations. The YMCA mission is described as "improving human life and helping people realize their fullest potential as children of God through development of spirit, mind, and body." The goals of the YMCA, in addition to providing care for latchkey children, is to support children's development through curricular activities that are physically and cognitively stimulating and adapted to individuals' needs. There is a great deal of choice, ample materials and equipment, and emphasis on outdoor play and arts and crafts.

The senior leader showed videotapes from the kits and suggested activities but was completely flexible about what the children did. With the science kit, she acted as a materials resource person; with the math kit, she became a facilitator and participant. Children became increasingly engaged in kit activities, working cooperatively and supportively. At this site, boys and girls seemed to prefer different activities. Both boys and girls liked the math activities, but girls became involved in more craft-like science activities, while boys preferred to go play outside.

Importance of the Leader

Perhaps the most important conclusion of both the observational study and the broad-based studies was that the group leader is a key factor in whether materials like the math and science kits are used successfully in after-school programs. However, the observational studies, in particular, also captured the fact that leaders do not work in a vacuum. Instead, each center has its own culture, formed by such factors as the mission and values of the sponsoring agency; the educational philosophies and beliefs of the leaders and their conception of the role that after-school programs should play; the needs of the particular children being served; the physical, intellectual, and financial resources of the site; and the structure, routine, and traditions of the programs. For example, centers staffed by licensed teachers tended to turn the activities into formal lessons, while centers that saw themselves as caretakers made minimal use of complex games (Inverness Research Associates, 1991).

Another conclusion of the studies concerns the ways the math and science kits were implemented. Many options exist for introducing educational programs into after-school settings, but the idea of doing math and science is foreign to the after-school culture (see also Brustel Corporation, 1991; Martin 1990). Most after-school program leaders see math and science as school subjects in which they are unprepared to lead. Thus, as the CTW math and science materials were introduced into the after-school programs, leaders perceived them in terms of existing program niches. That is, the Square One math materials were used during game time and were valued as games, irrespective of whether they were puzzles, hands-on activities, or board games.

They were not seen as a way to learn principles of mathematics. Similarly, the 3-2-1 Contact science activities were perceived as arts and crafts. The leaders focused on the activities in the kit that emphasized construction (for example, jewelry making) rather than science (for example, balloon rockets or bubbles), which the children liked very much but which leaders themselves did not quite understand. Sometimes 3-2-1 activities fit into a literacy niche, so leaders and children chose the activities in the kit that involved word games or puzzles (Inverness Research Associates, 1991).

Group leaders' lack of preparation for activities also limited the use of the kits. They rarely read the Leader's Guides or even game instructions. Most often, when the children were ready to start, the leaders opened the kit boxes and chose some activities for them to do (Inverness Research Associates, 1991; Hezel Associates, 1991; Katz, 1991). Leaders' lack of preparation led them consciously and unconsciously to steer the activities toward areas they knew well and with which they were relatively comfortable. So, when we did not see as much exploring, discovering, and playing around (that is, hands-on science) as we had hoped we concluded that such curiosity and exploration depends on leaders that understand the nature of inquiry. In the sites studied, leaders largely focused on procedure—on simply getting activities to happen—so that they ended up taking the shortest routes to helping children simply just do the activity. The idea of heightening the learning experience—by raising new questions and helping children pursue them—was quite foreign to almost all leaders. Under these conditions, it was not surprising that the leaders chose 3-2-1 activities that focused on arts and crafts (involving scissors, glue, and paper) rather than the exploration of natural phenomena (Inverness Research Associates, 1991).

Benefits of CTW After-School Materials

Overall, we found that children and leaders enjoyed the games and activities (Inverness Research Associates, 1991; Hezel Associates, 1991; Katz, 1991). In addition to providing fun, the math and science kits produced some other benefits for children. Social benefits accrued to both individuals and the group as a whole. First, we saw more than one example of a child who was a consistent behavior problem—that is, who had difficulty concentrating on activities or who disrupted other children's activities—finding a peaceful role with the CTW materials. The activities provided a chance for children to become engaged in something. It was apparent that the children craved activities in which they could immerse themselves. In these activities, they found challenges that could absorb and genuinely interest them.

The kits also provided many chances for children to practice cooperation. Particularly in the math games, children often evolved cooperative group practices, especially after they had played a game long enough to develop sound strategies. Children often shared strategies with each other, explaining why one would work more successfully than another. The object of the games shifted from winning to playing well, and children teamed up to beat the game rather than each other.

Second, in the best cases, the 3-2-1 Contact activities served as rich starting points for creative investigations and projects where kids worked together over extended periods of time, exploring, designing, and inventing. The math games led some of the older students to think about and discuss strategy. The kinds of strategies they discovered are found in many games (for example, gin rummy) but the children in our studies appeared to have little common experience with these other games. In playing Square One games, the children also became familiar with math vocabulary.

The kind of problem solving the children appeared to engage in is more associated with design, troubleshooting, and overcoming practical difficulties than it is with traditional notions of scientific or mathematical problem solving. The kind of learning that was most prevalent accrued from children's simply trying to make the activities work well. They learned to improvise when materials were lacking, to design when they had to invent new structures out of cardboard or modeling clay, and to communicate and cooperate, and so forth. For example, during a math board game that involves rolling dice, adding or multiplying their face values, and strategically placing tokens on the game board, the observer noted, "When it was obvious that everyone was doing the math for each roll, one boy reinforced the fairness rule: 'You can help each other with the math, but no telling where to go'" (Inverness Research Associates, 1991, p. H-9)

Third, in the sites that emphasized supporting the program participants' literacy and basic skills, the CTW materials gave children chances to practice various aspects of language such as talking, communicating, reading, spelling, and some writing. Leaders selected activities of this kind sometimes because they felt children needed reinforcement of a particular skill, and also, as we stated, because they were more comfortable with activities of this kind. Note that we never saw any kind of formal assessment of children's needs being undertaken in an after-school program.

Design Issues

The research of the Children's Television Workshop on SACC programs suggests that to succeed in the garden variety after-school environment, educational activities must be assimilable in critical ways (Brustel, 1991; Katz, 1990a; Maguire Associates, 1991; Martin, 1990; Martin and Shapiro, 1990; Research Communications, Ltd., 1990).

Materials must allow for choice. Activities in after-school centers are largely voluntary, and both children and programs have needs for different types of activity at different moments. Thus, materials must lead to a diverse and appealing array of activities that can be used independently of each other.

Activities should be flexible to allow for the wide range of ages and abilities among those who use them. Groups and individuals, younger children and older children, leader-led groups and independent groups each are active at different times in after-school settings.

Activities need to take a familiar form so they fit well into program niches. In particular, building around games, sports, creative activities, and literacy challenges is useful.

Materials that invite a child to participate by being readily usable and easy to initiate are important; yet they should go beyond the entry-level engagement to offer deeper levels to explore. Designs that allow children to gain mastery with repeated use are very desirable.

Finally, games should have good form; that is, they should be satisfying to play. Children seek out challenges that engage them.

Implications for SACC Programming

After-school care is an increasingly important and pervasive institution in the lives of U.S. children. Many children will spend over three thousand hours in a SACC program during their elementary years. The nature of these settings is being examined more closely by educators and communities who seek to meet children's needs during those informal but structured hours out of the home and school. Institutional responses to the need for child care range from bare but safe cafeterias with children idling, to elaborate facilities offering "courses," to one-on-one tutoring. In all these contexts, administrators and leaders are looking for good ideas for inexpensive, engaging activities that respect children's apparent need to be autonomous and relaxed. They would like to provide experiences for children that they may learn from and that open up the world a little for them or connect them to their communities in ways that schools are unable to do (Katz, 1990a; Martin, 1990; Martin and Shapiro, 1990).

Conclusion

By combining several kinds of evaluation with the materials development process, we are able to suggest some guidelines for increasing the effectiveness of the activities offered to children in after-school programs. We found that the materials that are most successful in a wide range of environments have the following characteristics (Inverness Research Associates, 1991):

Each set of activities offers children an appealing range of choices.

Activities are inviting to both individuals and groups of different ages, with or without leaders.

The form of the activities are familiar to children and leaders, so they can integrate them into existing routines.

The activities have appeal by virtue of their goals, their interactional possibilities, and their content.

While the activities allow easy entry, they also permit more sophisticated and richer experiences through repetition.

Educational researchers interested in after-school child care environments and the educational possibilities they offer have a number of choices (Collins, 1992). Perhaps the most natural impulse is to design special programs that make up for what children's school experiences lack. For example, some educators are producing remedial activities that are fun for children. An alternative design method starts with what the community says it needs and tries to support these needs with special programming, for example, by providing cultural programs that involve literacy skills. The CTW effort follows a third approach, which is to design materials that require little initial change in the way activities are routinely organized by SACC leaders. This latter approach allows materials to reach large numbers of programs. While it means accepting some limits on the ways that those materials are used, it also offers the possibility of creating incremental change in an important learning environment.

Appendix: Annotated List of Selected CTW Studies of After-School Environments and Materials

Not all of the following reports are available for circulation.

Brustel Corporation (1991). *After School Program Study*. Group interviews of forty-eight after-school group leaders in three cities about these leaders' content and format preferences for program materials.

Hezel Associates (1991). *Square One Superkit Field Test Final Report*. A three-month study of twenty-one after-school programs in Syracuse that used the CTW math kit.

Inverness Research Associates (1991). *A Study of CTW Kits in After School Settings*. A six-week case study of the use of CTW math and science kits in six after-school programs in three cities.

B. M. Katz (1990a). *Report on Phone Interviews Among After School Program Leaders*. Phone interviews with 130 after-school group leaders and administrators around the country about programs, facilities, resources.

B. M. Katz (1990b). *3-2-1 Contact Action Kit Mail Survey*. Surveys of reactions and suggestions of after-school group leaders and administrators in five states who reviewed prototypes of a CTW science kit.

B. M. Katz (1991). *Final Report on the Louisville Use Test of the 3-2-1 Action Kit*. A three-month study among twenty-five after-school programs in Louisville that used the CTW math kit.

Maguire Associates (1991). *Assessment of After School Materials for the Literacy Project*. Group interviews of 116 leaders in four cities about literacy goals and activities in after-school programs and reactions to ideas for "Ghostwriter"-related materials.

L.M.W. Martin (1990). *Administrators' and Curriculum Specialists' Meeting, March 28, 1990*. Report on a day-long meeting of eight experts in after-school programs.

L.M.W. Martin and D. Shapiro (1990). *Square One Child Care Project: First Phase*

Results. Results of a test in which children and group leaders in four school-based after-school programs in the New York City area used a prototype CTW math kit, based on the Mathnet series used on "Square One TV."

Morrison and Morrison, Ltd. (1991). *3-2-1 Contact Action Kit Field Test Follow-Up Survey.* A year-end follow-up phone survey of twenty-two centers that participated in the Louisville field test of the CTW science kit.

Research Communications, Ltd. (1990). *Assessment of Square One Plus Video.* Report on a test in which nineteen school-based after-school group leaders and the children they work with used a CTW prototype math kit based on segments from "Square One TV."

References

Armstrong, T. "The Power of Pretend." *Parenting,* Jan. 1990, pp. 30–31.

Brustel Corporation. *After School Program Study.* Report prepared for the Children's Television Workshop. Teaneck, N.J.: Brustel Corporation, 1991.

Collins, A. Remarks at the symposium "Is There Science and Math After School?" chaired by L. Martin, at the annual meeting of the American Educational Research Association, San Francisco, Apr. 1992.

Dyrud, C. *School-Age Child Care Programs in Oregon.* Salem, Oreg.: Department of Education, 1989.

Hezel Associates. *Square One Superkit Field Test Final Report.* Report prepared for the Children's Television Workshop. Syracuse, N.Y.: Hezel Associates, 1991.

Inverness Research Associates. *A Study of CTW Kits in After School Settings.* Report prepared for the Children's Television Workshop. Inverness, Calif.: Inverness Research Associates, 1991.

Katz, B. M. *Report on Phone Interviews Among After School Program Leaders.* Report prepared for the Children's Television Workshop. Louisville, Ky.: B. M. Katz, 1990a.

Katz, B. M. *3-2-1 Contact Action Kit Mail Survey.* New York: Children's Television Workshop, 1990b.

Katz, B. M. *Final Report on the Louisville Use Test of the 3-2-1 Action Kit.* Report prepared for the Children's Television Workshop. Louisville, Ky.: B. M. Katz, 1991.

Maguire Associates. *Assessment of After School Materials for the Literacy Project.* Report prepared for the Children's Television Workshop. Concord, Mass.: Maguire Associates, 1991.

Martin, L.M.W. *Administrators' and Curriculum Specialists' Meeting, March 28, 1990.* New York: Children's Television Workshop, 1990.

Martin, L.M.W., and Shapiro, D. *Square One Child Care Project: First Phase Results.* New York: Children's Television Workshop, 1990.

Marx, F. "School-Age Child Care in America: Ten Years Later." *Research Report,* 1990, *9* (2). (Wellesley, Mass.: Wellesley College Center for Research on Women.)

Morrison and Morrison, Ltd. *3-2-1 Contact Action Kit Field Test Follow-Up Survey.* Louisville, Ky.: Morrison and Morrison, Ltd., 1991.

New York State Council on Children and Families. *School Age Child Care: A Continuing Series of Technical Assistance Papers.* Washington, D.C.: ERIC Clearinghouse, Department of Education, May 1988. (ED 307 972)

Research Communications, Ltd. *Assessment of Square One Plus Video.* Report prepared for the Children's Television Workshop. Chestnut Hill, Mass.: Research Communications, Ltd., 1990.

Rogan, B., and Graves, S. *Who's Watching the Kids?* Report to the Alabama State Department of Education. Birmingham: University of Alabama, 1989.

School-Age Child Care Council. *Getting Started No. 4: Developing a Curriculum for School-Age Child Care*. Atlanta, Ga.: School-age Child Care Council, 1989.

LAURA MARTIN is vice president for production research at the Children's Television Workshop.

CAROL ASCHER is a senior research associate at Teachers College, Columbia University.

Inner-city, at-risk adolescents prefer organizations that provide a range of program choices, offer youth-driven activities, and permit high levels of activity and enjoyment.

The Project of Learning from the Inner-City Youth Perspective

Shirley Brice Heath

A battle that began soon after World War II still continues between the great majority who see schools as the primary place of learning for youths and the small minority who occasionally jump up to point out that more learning goes on out of schools than within them. In the past decade, some of the latter group have brought "everyday" learning to schools in the form of out-of-school or after-school programs. Not surprisingly, such opportunities (including most of those described in this volume) define themselves as additive, attempting to extend, build upon, and expand what takes place in classrooms. Animating such programs is the dual goal of improving student performance in school and altering teachers' ways of presenting and assessing knowledge. The elements that consistently enliven these after-school programs are collaborative projects, integration of subject areas within authentic activities, and extensive reflective writing by the young people themselves, particularly writing that includes planning and self-assessment. Apprenticeship to community artisans and business personnel, as well as mentoring relationships with adult program volunteers, provides the regular contact with adults who respect and care for youths that young people report they want (Carnegie Council on Adolescent Development, 1992).

Supported by the Spencer Foundation under a grant awarded to Shirley Brice Heath and Milbrey W. McLaughlin, this research project also included Merita A. Irby and Juliet Langman as senior research associates, working closely with teams formed from twenty junior ethnographers recruited from the youth organizations studied. Ali Calicotte and Steven Balt assisted in data collection and maintenance, and Jeffrey Lox managed the complex qualitative data sets and developed a computer program to analyze the language data.

Programs Studied

In the analyses reported in this chapter, I and the other researchers for this project looked at community-based programs that had no association with schools in order to determine what attracted youths and adults to these voluntary environments. We observed that programs attractive to inner-city youths fostered problem solving, reflective thinking, and strong self-image among these youths, who ranged in age from early adolescence into early adulthood. Over a five-year period, using anthropological field methods, we observed and recorded the language and activities of youth organizations located in the inner cities of three major metropolitan areas of the United States. We included only those youth organizations that local young people judged effective—places that offered activities and groups the youths voluntarily wanted to join. Youth organizations they selected included such groups as Girl Scouts; Boys and Girls Clubs; YMCA gang intervention programs; grassroots basketball, Little League, and tumbling teams; and storefront institutions that taught dance and drama. Our goal was to learn what happens within these organizations; we did so by coexisting, as unobtrusively as possible, in the midst of their activities for extended periods of time and by incorporating members of the groups into our research teams to serve as data collectors and to participate in discussions and analyses of findings.

We observed the groups through all phases of their activities, recording in field notes as much as possible about nonverbal actions, physical placement, and use of equipment. In addition, we recorded and transcribed the language that accompanied the actions and applied several types of discourse analysis to the resulting million-word corpus. Beyond our relatively unobtrusive ways of collecting data, we asked questions informally during activity downtimes. Throughout the research, we occasionally conducted more formal interviews to ensure that members of teams and their adult leaders had a chance to respond to the same questions. We also interviewed outsiders such as funders, social service personnel, and local civic and juvenile justice leaders about their understanding of what went on within the effective youth organizations and their reasons for supporting these organizations. All respondents were aware of our keen interest in the tough questions of how and what youths learned in the activities of the youth organizations they voluntarily attended.

Life in the Effective Organization

As described more fully in Heath and McLaughlin (1993) and McLaughlin, Irby, and Langman (1994), the learning environments of our selected youth groups exhibited certain macro- and micro-organizational features that reflected the beliefs of the adult leaders.

Mutual Understandings. Above all, the organizations provided a safe place where youngsters were protected from physical and emotional harm and shared responsibility for decisions about group activities and daily work in those activities. Adults actively sought out the advice of young people and involved them in planning, implementation, and evaluation. Leaders were strongly committed to tough discipline, high standards, and group interdependence as promoting excellence in individual achievement. Within each youth organization, the life of the group was marked by cycles of production, with planning, preparation, practice, performance, and evaluation of an activity usually covering nine weeks to three months. Though performance centered around a single activity, such as basketball or drama, important processes like problem solving, identifying and collecting resources, and developing mutual support among team members went on within each phase of the cycle. Dependent on a diversity of talents and abilities to meet the wide-ranging needs of their generally underfunded and understaffed organizations, adults regarded young people as resources and assets, not as problems or liabilities.

During the planning stage, adult leaders laid out general parameters of the cycle ahead, asked a few questions, and then left it to the youths to ask questions and propose ideas. Older youths, familiar with this phase, usually began tossing out ideas while younger ones listened. During preparation, which extended throughout the practice/rehearsal season or term, younger and older group members alike were brought into the search for resources and the consideration of special problems. Often, adult leaders stepped in during the preparation period to remind a group that such planned events as performances, field trips, and tournaments might be jeopardized unless certain needs were met first. Moreover, the adult leaders consistently reminded youngsters that the leaders could not make things happen without the help of the youths. Throughout each cycle, older youths often assumed responsibility for the instruction of younger members. In practice, leaders insisted youngsters play a variety of roles and positions, so that they could know intimately the strategies and movements of other members of the troupe or team. Members of athletic groups practiced in all positions—catcher, pitcher, or shortstop, forward or guard. Members of dramatic troupes shifted roles for each skit or play, playing a variety of characters and explaining the motives, movements, and expressions of each. Each specific activity took place within a framework of strict discipline codes that were minimal in number but maximal in their impact. No member of any group was allowed to bring or use drugs, weapons, or gang colors; breaking one of these rules meant suspension from activities or exclusion from the group. Responsibility for other members of the group and for group property belonged to everyone. Signs of disrespect or loss of concern for the continuing high-quality competitiveness of the group met swift censure and warnings; repeated infractions brought warnings, with expulsion for those who did not follow group norms. Since many of these youth organizations had limited memberships and long waiting lists, individuals who participated long enough to sense what being part of the group meant rarely risked expulsion; second chances for reentry were by no means guaranteed.

Authentic Assessment. Learning in the organizations that attracted youths centered on group-endorsed projects; the group planned, prepared, and

practiced for summative performances that took place before outside evaluators. For example, Little League teams faced playoffs and tournaments knowing that umpires, onlookers, and other coaches and teams would be their
judges, and that any personal quirks, excuses, and idiosyncrasies would not
be viewed tolerantly in the group's performance before these assessor strangers.
Similarly, dance and drama teams knew they had to face reviews of their final
performances before local cable television crews and viewers, parks and recreation groups, or local schools and clubs who might be harsh or critical.

In addition to performance assessments, certain groups employed more
traditional pencil-and-paper tests of content knowledge. For example, a Boys
and Girls Club summer drama program gave a formal written examination at
the end of the summer after a variety of experts had instructed youngsters daily
on topics that the program members addressed in their scripts. In order to
write scripts about cults, drugs, or sexually transmitted diseases, youngsters
heard from neurologists, gynecologists, chemists, law enforcement officials,
psychiatrists, and mental health counselors, and they read materials about such
areas of local relevance as social services distribution and state and county
laws. Program participants had to pass the written test on these materials with
a score of 90 or above at the end of the summer in order to continue with the
next stage of the program—weekly performances before local schools and
youth groups.

A grass-roots dance and acting group under contract to provide end-of-
summer performances for a city parks and recreation program called for a similar integration of the diverse ways of displaying competence. Youngsters
turned in daily journals offering music suggestions, script samples, and reflections on practice and rehearsal. Using anatomy charts, they documented
changing patterns of sore muscles as dance routines increased in difficulty and
intensity. Music lessons surrounding the groups' choosing instruments to
accompany their performance included the history of particular kinds of
music, the principles of physics at work in various types of drums, and the
mathematics behind musical notation.

As part of a philosophy that learning counts, programs often strongly
emphasized keeping up school grades, preparing for standardized tests during
the school year, and doing homework. Some after-school programs insisted
that youngsters spend some time doing homework before they could practice
for their athletic or arts events with other group members. Many programs
offered tutoring as part of their array of activities and counted on volunteers
to maintain one-on-one relationships with youngsters in order to keep them
motivated to do well in school and to face tests there with positive attitudes.

Interactions and Reflective Practices. Small slices of behavior within
the organizations, individuals interacting with individuals, mirrored behaviors
at the organizational level. The amount and type of language used between
adult leaders and youths differed within each phase of the activity cycle, as did
the amount of direct action. During planning and early practice stages, adults
asked a high percentage of open-ended questions, set up hypothetical situa-

tions for youths to consider, and projected scenarios of the teams' upcoming practice and performance events. Similarly, youths who worked with younger children during practices asked them to reflect on what they were doing at particular points in a dramatic scene or practice baseball game, for example, and they frequently stopped practice to ask younger children to describe what had just happened and to speculate on ways to improve or redirect what had just occurred.

During the early phases of practice, adults peppered their talk with "what if," "how about," and "if . . . then" phrases, throwing out hypothetical scenes and sequences of events for the youths to consider. They asked questions that called on youths to explain what they were doing with parts of their body at particular points, how they felt in a particular stance, and what was going on in their heads. These probing questions were not designed to be indirect directives or satirical comments to learners. They were consistent with a continuous emphasis on thinking, on remembering, and on staying alert at all times to what was going on in the immediate environment. As a cycle moved toward final performance or tournament competition, hypothetical talk and explanatory verbal reminders by adult leaders were supplanted by more talk from youngsters, such as questions of clarification and reassessments of particular routines. In the final weeks of a cycle, adult talk again prevailed, but now in brief, running comments and directives during final practices and rehearsals, often addressed to specific team members ("nice going," "good play, Joey," "downstage, Rachel, downstage"). Joking, jesting, and playing around marked work sessions as well as periods of travel to and from practices or performances. Adults and youngsters alike often developed nicknames for each other, and sometimes special codes for cheers or pep talks emerged within the groups. Both adults and young people wore special pieces of clothing and insignia to mark their status within the group. All adult members of each organization—whether custodians, managers, receptionists, coaches, or board members—counted as full members and, once accepted by the youths, expected respectful and mannerly behavior and language from those youths.

Youth Organizations as Border Zones

The inner-city youth organizations we studied served as border zones between life on the streets and life in mainstream institutions of education and employment. Both adults and youths acknowledged this zone as a safe place to practice and reflect on what it meant in both worlds to compete to survive, to develop tactical means of competing and surviving, and to balance individual interests and group goals. Familiar with life on the streets, the youths needed few explications of what survival there meant: acting tough, "hanging" with those who could be trusted, and constantly weighing the benefits and costs of particular choices and actions. But with certain adaptations, these same rules applied in the mainstream world, along with particular norms related to ways of talking, dressing, respecting protocol, gaining and acting on information, and asking for clarification. Thus, the effective youth organizations emphasized punctuality, neatness, politeness, and standard English language forms and habits of discourse, as well as specific technical skills, such as those surrounding electronic recording equipment and computers. Young members often worked within their organizations in a variety of positions that reinforced not only the skills, but also the attitudes and language necessary to meet the public. They served as receptionists, clerical help, publicists, and junior counselors. In addition, they received praise for their ability to remember facts and terms, know something about community resources and consumer economics, and display competence typical of particular occupations ranging from disc jockey to carpenter to travel guide. Resolution of problems ranging from racist incidents to breach of contract cases came up often in the youth organizations, creating opportunities for youths to reflect on ways to handle such problems without conflict but with firm pride and resolve.

The youth organizations we observed helped youngsters acknowledge schools as places where they had to survive much that was unfair, unreasonable, and sometimes cruel while remaining determined to earn their high school diplomas. Talk often turned to what youngsters could and could not expect of standardized testing programs, employment counselors, police officers, employers, city officials, and members of the juvenile justice system. Adult leaders argued that the organizational evaluators—the umpires, referees, audiences, and public—that the youngsters met during travel for performances were just like the other evaluators the young people would meet in the world outside the inner city. Injustice, racism, discrimination, irrational demands, and blind-side assaults were always potentially present and unpredictable. Therefore, the young people had to work together to learn to compete more successfully, both as team members for their organization and as individuals within the mainstream arenas of education and employment. In addition, they needed to recognize the value of reflection, talking things out, and thinking about long-term consequences and implications for the group before acting as individuals.

Work as a Reality

The need the youths would soon have for employment and the possibility of their attending college permeated their inner-city organizations. The primary metaphor for their central activities, from basketball to swimming to drama, was work. Tasks were performed that allowed the youths to use skills in language, mathematics, filing, map reading, and writing in order to complete some activity, but adults also spoke often of their own need to use these kinds of skills in their adult lives as workers and as family members.

For the most part, team members anchored their relationships and activities in their project, performance, or end-of-season playoffs. They knew they had to perfect the specific segments of action and production that accompanied each part of the project, and they had to prepare for the performance by collecting the necessary physical resources—often both spatial and material.

Along with this team work on a group project, participants also needed to think about ways to improve their individual performances or better their own records in order to contribute to the team's advancement. Such interdependence was often likened by adult leaders to the way it is on the job in the mainstream world, where an individual's increased skills, confidence, and information helps an entire group accomplish its goals. In the absence of jobs in the U.S. labor force for inner-city youths, their work within youth organizations provided not only valuable experience, but also content for building resumés, references, and a base of knowledge to draw from in employment interviews. Adult leaders of youth organizations served as guidance and employment counselors, information and service brokers, and references for group members. In the majority of cases, work within youth organizations provided the only extracurricular life youngsters could refer to as they detailed their personae on applications for further education and employment.

Learning in Youth Organizations

Looking inside these inner-city organizations reveals what happens in after-school learning that inner-city young people themselves value. Youngsters who remained in the programs more than one season reported an increase in self-control and self-respect, greater ability to find ways around the criminal and violent activities of their neighborhoods, and stronger hopes and expectations for their own futures. All reported their belief that involvement in the program had helped them stay in school, find friends who also wanted to stay in school, and link with a caring adult who served as role model. Along with good times, good friends, and a safe place to be, their youth organizations offered one highly special side benefit in the eyes of young people; that was travel, which allowed them, as one of them said, the chance "to see things and to get to know all sorts of people."

One goal of our research was to determine how learning takes place within youth organizations that carry no formal alliance with schools. In these programs, macrostructural principles of mutual understanding and authentic assessment enabled microlevel interactional and reflective practices. Every member of a group was a resource needed within an array of activities and supported by firm rules and high expectations. Key events such as games or performances contained split-second representations of larger structural arrangements and principles of interaction. For example, a winning shot in a basketball game emerged out of a series of assists that in turn resulted from skills and trust built among members during all their group activities. The real interactions, on the one hand, and the organizational ethos of youths working together and helping each other, on the other hand, bore a figure-and-ground relationship.

A stream of signals from overt statements of rules to nearly invisible codes of hand signals and body postures regulated, limited, and defined interactions behind everyday learning (Hanks, 1992; Kendon, 1992). Youngsters talked and acted within a context of positive, guiding language with ample demonstration and practice, seasonal cycles of preparation and practice culminating in a performance for outside evaluators, and cross-age, cross-situational coaching by youths of youths. All youngsters had opportunities to see themselves as both expert and learner, coach and coached, and participant in several slices of organizational life. Programs differed in the specific ways they enabled such interactions, but across the sixty organizations we studied, organizational structures and belief systems shaped the ebb and flow of routine daily life for young members. Assumptions about learning, rather than teaching, motivated each organization's activities and interactions. There were few similarities between teacher-driven, passive-student schooling and the active, lively, role-shifting, task-focused learning of these inner-city programs (compare Singleton, 1989).

All adults in the groups we studied encouraged youngsters to remain in school, and if the youngsters could not, then to consider finding some other way of continuing their education. As noted earlier, many programs provided homework support, academic tutoring and mentors, or special tutelage for particular tests, such as the Scholastic Aptitude Test or the GED examination. Some organizations were loosely connected to private schools or churches that offered middle school and high school scholarships for promising minority students; others included staff members with strong personal connections to historically black colleges or local community colleges likely to give athletic scholarships. Adults within these youth organizations consistently viewed schools as inhumane environments for urban youths, disconnected from the realities of the youths' worlds, and destructive of youths' self-images. Many—among them former schoolteachers—saw their present jobs as undoing in the afternoons what schools had done to the young people during the day. It was not uncommon for the adults to lament that "all [the youths] hear all day is how bad they are. We can't even begin [our work in the youth center] until we can make them feel okay, good about themselves." Some saw schools as treating youngsters as "invisible—just not there." Other youth leaders regretted that schools resisted creating conditions in which students could search for answers and raise their own questions through authentic tasks. Thus, though they supported homework, academic achievement, and high school completion, youth organizations took special care to make certain they would not be too closely identified with schools and, hence, linked to the uncaring and unknowing attitudes that neighborhood parents and youths characterized as typical of local schools.

Newly created after-school learning programs may benefit from comparative studies (such as the research reported here) of existing programs that are, though not designed as experiments, functioning as experiments. What we saw was that the voluntary contexts of youth organizations demand authenticity, apprenticeship, and integration of subject areas such as I described earlier if they are to attract and retain youths. Organizational structures meshed with and supported the micro-features of specific learning situations so that learners came to know what to expect, both of the group and of themselves. Such expectations came not just from being told but from direct experience acquired through the variety of organizational roles that youngsters played. In addition to this participatory involvement, youngsters also heard much about the similarity between their membership within a youth group and participation in the larger society; youths and their leaders also often thought aloud about the contrasts and similarities between the rules for survival in their neighborhoods with the norms of the youth organization and mainstream educational and employment institutions. Motivation for the individual meshed closely with the rise and fall of group performance. What may be termed the culture of the group shaped schemas that individuals developed to guide their behaviors (D'Andrade, 1992).

These critical elements that we observed may be the key to the organizations' judged effectiveness, enabling the kind of sustained learning urban youngsters report from their organizational involvement. Moreover, much of what occurs in these groups fits with current theories of development that stress participatory apprenticeships that incorporate both immediate task- or performance-centered learning and awareness of the group's historical and social circumstances (Lave and Wenger, 1991; Rogoff, 1993). Youth organization alumni and older members report that they not only recall and use information and experience gained from their organizations but also find themselves in similar planning, preparing, practicing, and evaluating situations in their work and family lives. For them, the incessant talk, practice, and evaluation within the youth organizations added up to learning that they could transfer and adapt to other events in their lives, primarily mainstream education and training, work, and interactions with bureaucratic organizations. In addition, youth group members see themselves as constantly learning, modeling, and instructing even outside the organization. They take responsibility for younger neighborhood children and see it as their task, as one said, to "give the little ones somebody to be there for them." Effective youth programs insist on youngsters' doing, thinking, and helping others learn in order to show these youngsters how to bring their skills and knowledge to bear in a host of roles within and beyond the organization.

Comparisons across learning environments must continue to rethink context (Duranti and Goodwin, 1992), bringing together ethnographic techniques of long-term interactive fieldwork with theories that increase researchers' understanding of ways to analyze language and context as interdependent. This perspective will focus not only on spoken language, but also on other symbol systems prevalent in both play and work, such as demonstration through gesture or mime. A youngster's learning in various phases of development and of different types of content knowledge and skills depends on his or her being embedded within activities as well as able to project the self visually and mentally into certain roles. It will take interdisciplinary work in settings beyond those typically associated with teaching to advance educators' and adult leaders' understanding of such learning. To grasp the active role of the learner, they need much more knowledge than is now available about ways that self-efficacy and motivation increase for individuals as they participate in group projects that have high content, skill, and performance demands. All those concerned with children's development especially need to consider learning contexts and activities for children beyond the preschool years in programs and groups these youths themselves seek out and choose for sustained involvement.

References

Carnegie Council on Adolescent Development. *A Matter of Time: Risk and Opportunity in the Nonschool Hours*. New York: Carnegie Corporation of New York, 1992.

D'Andrade, R. "Schemas and Motivation." In R. D'Andrade and C. Strauss, *Human Motives and Cultural Models*. New York: Cambridge University Press, 1992.

Duranti, A., and Goodwin, C. (eds.). *Rethinking Context: Language as an Interactive Phenomenon*. New York: Cambridge University Press, 1992.

Hanks, W. F. "The Indexical Ground of Deictic Reference." In A. Duranti and C. Goodwin (eds.), *Rethinking Context: Language as an Interactive Phenomenon*. New York: Cambridge University Press, 1992.

Heath, S. B., and McLaughlin, M. W. *Identity and Inner-City Youth: Beyond Ethnicity and Gender*. New York: Teachers College Press, 1993.

Kendon, A. "The Negotiation of Context in Face-to-Face Interaction." In A. Duranti and C. Goodwin (eds.), *Rethinking Context: Language as an Interactive Phenomenon*. New York: Cambridge University Press, 1992.

Lave, J., and Wenger, E. *Situated Learning: Legitimate Peripheral Participation*. New York: Cambridge University Press, 1991.

McLaughlin, M. W., Irby, M. A., and Langman, J. *Urban Sanctuaries: Neighborhood Organizations in the Lives and Futures of Inner-City Youth*. San Francisco: Jossey-Bass, 1994.

Rogoff, B. "Observing Sociocultural Activity on Three Planes: Participatory Appropriation, Guided Participation, Apprenticeship." In A. Alvarez, P. del Rio, and J. V. Wertsch (eds.), *Perspectives on Sociocultural Research*. New York: Cambridge University Press, 1993.

Singleton, J. "Japanese Folkcraft Pottery Apprenticeship: Cultural Patterns of an Educational Institution." In M. W. Coy (ed.), *Apprenticeship: From Theory to Method and Back Again*. Albany: State University of New York Press, 1989.

SHIRLEY BRICE HEATH is professor of English and linguistics, with courtesy appointments in anthropology and education, at Stanford University.

This chapter shows how a multisite, community-based computer-oriented after-school program facilitated the development of bilingual and computer literacy skills as well as other school-related skills among diverse groups of adolescents.

A Computer-Oriented After-School Activity: Children's Learning in the Fifth Dimension and La Clase Mágica

Miriam W. Schustack, Catherine King,
Margaret A. Gallego, Olga A. Vásquez

In this chapter, we describe a multisite, interdisciplinary project that examines and encourages literacy in school-age children who attend community-based after-school programs. We begin with a brief overview of the project, which is called the Fifth Dimension and which takes its form from the context within which it is embedded. Our Spanish-English bilingual-multicultural sites, reflecting the bilingual-bicultural characteristics of the communities in which they are located, are called La Clase Mágica, "The Magical Class." We next discuss the theoretical rationale and important features of our approach and review the efforts to evaluate our program. We briefly discuss our relationships to schools and to schooling and conclude with a discussion of our research consortium's evolving interdisciplinary collaborations.

We in this research consortium believe that our computer-mediated after-school activity, in addition to furthering understanding of how literacy is acquired and used, provides a promising avenue for youth-serving professionals to promote higher levels of basic and technological literacy in the pluralistic, multicultural society of the United States. Our major goal is to explore the effects

The work reported in this chapter is supported by a grant from the Andrew J. Mellon Foundation. We thank Michael Cole, Patricia Worden, Bill Blanton, and our other colleagues in the Distributed Literacy Consortium for comments on our drafts. Correspondence concerning this chapter should be sent to Miriam Schustack, Psychology Program, California State University, San Marcos, San Marcos, CA 92096-0001.

of a structured after-school computer club on literacy, and the development of children's academically relevant skills within the club's system of structured activity. Children's socially constructed understanding of technology and development of skills in planning and self-regulation are also among our concerns.

Our program's six primary research sites involve child and adult participants varying in age, ethnicity, primary language, socioeconomic status, and educational level. Site locations range from inner-city urban communities to affluent suburbs spread across the United States, and there is an affiliated site in Russia. Although different sites have somewhat varied research goals, these goals are complementary within the framework of our shared agenda. Each research site consists of an after-school program serving children between six and twelve years old. In the program, game playing and other playful activities engage children in meaningful oral and written communication and other educationally relevant activity. Computers are the main media for both games and written communication. The sites are located within existing after-school centers in Boys and Girls Clubs, schools, community-based centers, and churches. A major feature of the sites is adult-to-child and child-to-child interaction. Adult participants include university students and faculty as well as volunteer and paid community workers who engage in joint activity with the children.

The after-school programs are structured but not rigid, imposing varying degrees of constraint appropriate to the children's activity. We try to avoid an overly school-like environment in appearance, activities, and social roles. The children write frequent letters to children at other sites and to a jointly imagined mythical character of uncertain gender known as the Wizard (El Maga at the Spanish-English sites), whom we all conspire to present as the creator and ruler of the Fifth Dimension.

Theoretical Rationale

Our guiding theoretical idea, derived from the work of Dewey and Vygotsky, is that learning is grounded in activity and must be studied developmentally (Dewey, 1916; Vygotsky, 1978; Engestrom and Punamiki, 1993). In this view, children's learning occurs as an integral part of a set of activities that are coherent, rich, and appealing to children. The Fifth Dimension, with its own rules, artifacts, and relationships among participants, constitutes the activity system within which learning can occur. Thus, our program is structured to embody the principles of activity-based learning that occurs in its own legitimate context (compare Nicolopoulou and Cole, in press). The activity system is guided by four components: play mixed with education, writing and telecommunication, the construction of shared knowledge, and the situating of the activities in the community.

Play Mixed with Education. We deliberately mix play with education by involving children as active participants in a fantasy world ruled by an electronic being who magically oversees the functioning of that world, the Fifth Dimension. Along with varying amounts of overtly educational content, there are substantial opportunities for peer interaction in joint play. All the activities (and the structures that organize the children's movement among the activities) involve play, either through the activities' game-like structure or by their role in the fantasy world of the Fifth Dimension. Each child moves a little figurine through a physical maze to represent his or her path through Fifth Dimension activities. In each room of the maze are the names of two or three games, and the child can choose to play any of the games in the room where his or her figurine is located. Each game can be played at three levels (beginner, good, and expert), with game-specific criteria for achieving each level. The higher the level achieved in a game, the more options the child has for what to play next. In addition to a variety of computer games, noncomputer activities are available according to site needs and resources.

The most important theoretical consideration underlying this mixed activity system is that the primary attractions and rewards of participation are intrinsic to the activity; the children engage in specific computer—and non-computer—activities because they are enjoyable, and the children follow the rules in moving from one activity to another because the rules are central to the fantasy Fifth Dimension. One of our aims is to avoid the problems of the extrinsic reward structures (especially grades) that dominate school learning and to give the child a greater role in selecting activities. On a practical level, our reliance on voluntary participation requires that the activities remain rewarding so that children will continue to come. Because most of our sites offer competing recreational opportunities, the children will not participate in the Fifth Dimension unless they (or their parents) feel that it is fun as well as worthwhile.

The use of computers as a central artifact serves two agendas. First, computers can support educational elements of activities (games, reading, writing, and telecommunication) and can be a natural medium for organizing children's written communication. Second, computer-mediated activities allow children to gain familiarity with computers in a nonthreatening, nonevaluative environment. We emphasize computer-based activities that include such patently educational activities as programming and such patently playful activities as arcade-style games, as well as a great many educational games with both serious content and game structures (for example, the computer geography game Where in the World Is Carmen San Diego?). We encourage the children to collaborate with their adult partners in the hands-on computer activity, doing as much as they can of such tasks as booting machines, inserting diskettes, and setting game parameters that precede the actual writing or game playing.

The prominence of the fantasy features of the Fifth Dimension contributes to the sites' playful atmosphere. The Wizard, the maze, and other Fifth Dimension artifacts help to create a rich and coherent activity system whose effects on participating children can be evaluated.

Writing and Telecommunication. Writing activities are a major component of our programs. Each Fifth Dimension site is electronically linked to all the other sites as well as to the Wizard. Children from each site communicate individually and in groups with the Wizard and with pen pals at our other primary sites and at loosely affiliated similar sites as far away as Moscow. Writing activities center around electronic mail and a computer bulletin board although children also write using noncomputer media. The links between our sites are important because we believe that if children in different centers become interested in one another, we gain an additional intrinsic motive for the children's literate activity. By introducing children from different communities and allowing a real need and desire to communicate to develop, we provide the children with authentic reasons for writing; we make writing a grounded and purposeful activity rather than an abstract exercise. In addition, the researchers, undergraduates, and community workers at the different sites use electronic mail both for their own messages to other sites and for facilitating the correspondence between the children at different sites.

Writing activity is heavily structured around communication with the Wizard. Writing a letter to the Wizard is a requirement for completing many of the game activities within the maze, and aspects of the letter's content may be specified. For example, the instructions for finishing a game of Botanical Gardens may say, "Write a letter to the Wizard explaining how you figured out which environment makes the Donkey's Breath plant grow the tallest." The Wizard is a reliable correspondent, promptly answering every letter through the hidden mediation of the site staff. Thus, the child learns that every written communication to the Wizard will be rewarded with a reply from an encouraging, engaging, responsive partner. The Wizard provides the child with a model for good letters in terms of form (letter structure, language, spelling) and content (responsiveness to the needs, interests, and concerns of the letter writer). For example, El Maga is bilingual and writes letters in Spanish, English, or a mixture of both, as appropriate for the individual child. At most sites, children write approximately one letter to the Wizard each day they are at the site, and they spend roughly one-tenth to one-half of their time in the Fifth Dimension on writing (the amount of time depends on both the site and the individual child's interest in writing).

Construction of Shared Knowledge. An important part is played in our activities by those we call wizard's assistants (*amigos* and *amigas* at Spanish-English sites), adults acting as older siblings to the children. At most sites, this role is filled by university undergraduates, at the rest by nonstudent adults from the community and/or high-school students. On any given day, the number of adults at each site varies from two to fifteen while the number of children who visit varies from three to thirty-five. The adults' participation simultaneously provides several resources and satisfies several competing demands on our system. By their actions, the adults demonstrate that reading is a process of interpreting the world using text, that computers are to be enjoyed and not feared, and that planning and strategy selection are worthwhile activities. The adults (and the teenagers) are much admired by the children, providing role models not only in terms of literacy and problem-solving skills but in terms of social behavior as well.

We make certain, though, that our activities give the children legitimate opportunities to gain authority in their interactions with adults. For example, a child often is more expert at a game than the participating adult, which allows many opportunities for the child to take the lead role in joint play with the adult. At the sites where the wizard's assistants are undergraduates, the adults are largely a new group each academic semester or quarter and, thus, often not familiar with the games while many of the children do know the games through prior exposure at the site or elsewhere. Very often, a genuine division of labor is required because the children are more skilled at the mechanics of the activity than the adults, while the adults are better at forming strategies and keeping the larger goals in mind. This activity configuration provides flexible "zones of proximal development," a term we adopted from the work of Vygotsky and his students (Luria, 1979; Vygotsky, 1978; Rogoff and Wertsch, 1984; Griffin and Cole, 1984). As the adults use their interactions with the children to provide the scaffolding that allows the children to build more advanced understandings, the children learn from the adults, but the adults also get the experience of learning from (and with) the children. In this way, our activities promote adult-child relationships that are less authoritarian than those in the schools. Our more egalitarian adult-child relationship is possible because we have assigned the highly authoritarian role in our sites to the Wizard. With the Wizard as the ultimate authority, both child and adult citizens of the Fifth Dimension are subject to rules and structures not of their own making, and the Wizard takes any criticism or blame. It is also the Wizard who dispenses favors and special privileges and who settles disputes about the rules.

In general, the relationships formed through joint child-adult play in the Fifth Dimension foster the co-construction of knowledge. Even though the adults vary in age, education, ethnicity, and so forth, all of them are in a position to learn through their interactions with the children. The reversal of traditional power roles that comes about when the child knows more about an activity than the adult can have beneficial consequences for the child in terms of self-esteem and his or her understanding of social roles. It also has a more direct and practical benefit in giving the child a legitimate need to organize and present his or her own representation of the game. Such overt reflective activity can raise the level of the child's own understanding of the game and enhance the child's role in directing his or her own learning. Even when a child has great skill and success in a game, it is a challenge for the child to convey that expertise to another, and the child can become more aware of his or her own strategies and approaches by being required to verbalize them (or, at least, express them in some medium that can be shared, through a diagram, perhaps, or through pointing). This same beneficial self-reflection can occur when a child assumes the role of the more knowledgeable, capable participant in interaction with a peer. The powerful sense of having valued information to share with an admired other is all the stronger when the child can teach someone who is usually more knowledgeable, an adult who is usually in the role of authority.

On the adult's side of the interaction, there are opportunities for a broadened notion of expertise, a better understanding of the child as learner, and an increased genuine respect for the child's mastery of the domain.

When adult and child learn a game new to both, mutually beneficial interactions engage both. Constructing an intersubjective understanding of the activity gives them many opportunities to learn about one another's skills. In particular, this activity provides an appropriate time for the adult to demonstrate (in an unforced, genuine, task-appropriate manner) the usefulness of general problem-solving skills. The child can observe and participate in the kinds of reasoning and systematic experimentation that adults tend to engage in; this is especially true when the adult is able to comment on his or her actions as they occur. The joint learning situation seems most powerful in its potential to expose the child to concrete examples of applying advanced reasoning and problem-solving skills to a new situation.

When an adult engages in joint play with a child, he or she is faced with the challenge of deciding exactly what questions to ask in order to promote, support, and organize the child's developing understanding of the task. In our program, the adults are encouraged to facilitate children's learning by posing the right questions, and they learn that asking the right questions requires a much deeper understanding of tasks and of children's current knowledge than does simply providing answers to children's questions or showing children what to do. The adults acquire a better understanding of learning as they collaborate with the children to facilitate the children's learning.

Situating Activities in the Community. We find many benefits to situating our program after school. The children tend to sense that the community settings belong to them in a way that schools do not, so they feel a greater sense of ownership of activities in community settings than they do of school activities. Thus, we move learning (especially learning about technology) to environments where participants feel ownership, with the expectation that they will feel more strongly than they otherwise might that the skills they learn and the technology they use belong to them as well. Moreover, the skills of interest to the Fifth Dimension project make elementary-age children an appropriate focus for our efforts. The middle childhood years may be a sensitive period for the acquisition of some of the cognitive skills of interest to us, either because these skills are part of the school curriculum for children of this age or for maturational reasons (that is, the children's developmental stage may be especially suited to the learning experiences we offer). After-school settings tend to provide us with preferential access to that elementary school age group. Younger children tend not to be found in the open, free-choice environments of after-school centers, and older children are also less commonly found in these centers.

In addition to those benefits, we have a set of site-specific rationales for working in community settings. Primary among them is the possibility of creating an environment where Fifth Dimension activities can be made culturally relevant for the children of a particular community. For example, questions about the influence of bilingualism and multiculturalism on learning are prominent at our two Latino community sites (in Lansing, Michigan, and Solana Beach, California), and these questions show up in a different form at our two sites that primarily serve African American children (in New Orleans and Chicago). The focus on linguistic and cultural influence creates a context within which children's acquisition of cognitive skills can be more richly studied and the understanding of community-based literacy can be increased. Working within the community also allows our sites to apply local cultural perspectives when they are relevant to the knowledge and skills under study. For example, common storytelling activities in the child's home community differ according to whether that community is Spanish-speaking, African American, mostly white, or ethnically mixed. By working in culturally distinctive community settings, we can respond more appropriately to parental and community concerns.

In practice, after-school community-based settings also provide the flexibility that activities in the Fifth Dimension require. We are free from many constraints of accountability that we would face implementing our program within a school setting. We were also influenced to choose after-school settings by the notion that today's children need not only better quality education but also greater quantities of education; they need to use their nonschool time more productively to enhance the knowledge and skills they acquire in school (Carnegie Council on Adolescent Development, 1992). Our activity system also creates opportunities to spend greater time on a single task than is normally available in school.

Community-University Issues

In general, our arrangements with our host community settings have been mutually beneficial, although we have encountered occasional difficulties, primarily the difficulties inherent in setting up an environment conducive to good research as well as supportive of the targeted activities. Our goal is to find the appropriate balance between the demands of research and the realities of the after-school environment. Neither the tight control of a laboratory environment nor the usual chaos of loosely structured after-school recreation are suitable to our research. We try to find a point we think of as controlled chaos, which allows us to collect meaningful data while we keep the children motivated enough to continue participating. In practice, this means that Fifth Dimension settings tend to be noisy and busy places, where unplanned events unfold along with the organized ones and where activities are highly personalized. At sites located in recreational centers, we are imposing a more structured activity on a less structured environment. The Fifth Dimension does place more constraints on children's activities than many other programs the children could select. For example, in the Boys and Girls Clubs, the children can elect to spend time in unstructured activity in the game room or on the playground. They are accustomed to casually dropping in on the various activities and observing who is there and what is going on. This openness is positive in terms of the children's feeling of belonging, ownership, and choice, but it wreaks havoc with any attempts at systematic measurement of a child's level of participation.

A separate area of concern is how we researchers, as outsiders, can be perceived as part of the host institutions. The relationships that develop between Fifth Dimension staff and the children (as well as their parents) play a large role in our becoming integrated with our host institutions. Mutual exchange of support and knowledge between parents and Fifth Dimension staff helps build collaborative relationships. An important avenue for incorporation into the host institution opens up when host staff become strong supporters of our program, and our biggest promoters at many of our sites are just such staff. Although our current research activity is focused on observation and data gathering, the long-term agenda of this project also includes exploring whether the kinds of activity systems we create can be sustained and remain beneficial to the children without a strong ongoing university presence; we are thus vitally interested in gaining the support of the host institution for our activity. We pay close attention to the progress of institutionalization of the Fifth Dimension within our host settings and try to promote a sense of involvement on the part of the hosts. At some sites, the hosts pay part of the cost of Fifth Dimension staff—evidence of our success at integration.

Some difficulties for this research arise from our university settings as well. Sites where wizard's assistants are undergraduates are affected by the universities' curricula, and these sites do not follow the host institution's calendar, but the associated university's academic calendar. It is not in the best interest of the participating children (or of our research progress) that the Fifth Dimension is closed for many weeks, even though the host after-school center is open, but we are subject to the institutional constraints of the universities. In addition, the background experiences and disciplinary orientations of the undergraduate wizard's assistants can result in a mismatch between student attitudes and the objectives of the activity. For example, at our Michigan site, students come from a teacher education program and have expectations, roles, and behaviors typical of those who teach in formal schools. By contrast, the students at the San Marcos, California, site are primarily psychology majors who bring a focus on individual rather than socially constructed cognition, a focus derived from their training in traditional laboratory research. Regardless of their specific academic backgrounds, all the students also bring diverse individual attitudes about children, learning, and play, and interpret the research goals and their roles in individual ways. Such differences are not necessarily problems, but they do influence the character of each site and the nature of the adult-child interactions.

Additional institutional difficulties arise from the bureaucratic entanglements of conducting university research outside the university. Some are the minor inconveniences that affect any field research, but some are more a consequence of our complex interdependency with our hosts and, thus, are not always easily managed. For example, at many sites, equipment is shared in both directions between host and Fifth Dimension activities. The situation is fairly simple when the sharing is just a matter of different users on different days (that is, the hosts use Fifth Dimension computers for other activities when we are not there, and we use host computers during Fifth Dimension sessions).

But more complex questions arise when the issue is who should (or who can) pay for repairs, or when ownership is intermingled. If our computer is hooked up to their monitor, what moves when a project changes location? Given that both our project and our host institutions have tight budgets, there is not much room for simple and magnanimous solutions.

The positive side of the relationships between the universities and the host institutions in the community comes when the two kinds of institutions can form a synergistic system and we can work on coordinating the institutions for mutual benefit. For example, we make it easy for undergraduates to get involved by making their participation a regular part of their college education. This can be done, of course, only with the universities' consent and support. Students enroll in a regular credit-bearing course that includes basic theoretical work (readings and class discussions), training in writing field notes on observations of the children, and participation at the after-school site. In this way, we provide the universities with a rare form of research practicum class (offered within different disciplines at different universities) that is much in demand. Also, many universities have begun to acknowledge their obligations to their local communities and are supportive of students' performing community service. When we provide a concrete opportunity for students to get involved in a community-based program, the university benefits from the goodwill of the community, the program benefits from the free labor, and the children benefit from their extensive exposure to college students as role models and friends, a tremendously valuable experience for the large proportion of our children whose home settings have no college-educated adults.

Evaluating Program Effects

In our day-to-day on-site experience, we see indications of our success with the children and the community, and we are exploring a variety of approaches to evaluate how children are influenced by their participation in Fifth Dimension activity and to get reliable and valid measurement of program effects. We will discuss the methodological issues prominent in this research (involving embedded measurement and the selection of control groups) and then describe our findings on the children's level of mastery within the games and their performance in the specific skill and knowledge domains that we have studied: writing, computer literacy, and language.

Embedding Measurement in Activities. One of the most pressing methodological goals we have is to embed measurement into the children's ongoing activity, making measurement as invisible to the children as possible. Our data collection becomes a natural part of the activity; children can feel like Fifth Dimension citizens rather than research subjects or classroom pupils. To achieve this goal, we exploit the structured nature of our activities, so that the activities themselves provide most of the data we want to collect, minimizing separate testing activities. For example, at most of our sites, the central organizing structure for Fifth Dimension games is the maze, of approximately twenty "rooms," with a few games residing in each room. Each game has an associated task card that describes how to play the game and defines what must be done to reach each of the three possible levels of success. As we mentioned earlier, when a game is completed, the child has choices of which room to enter next, with the breadth of choice dependent on the level of expertise attained in the previous game. With the help of a wizard's assistant, children track their progress through the maze using a journey log, a paper form that records each game the child plays and what level is reached, and that journey log also serves as the main research record of the activities the child participated in on each visit to the Fifth Dimension, how long the child spent on each activity, and the level of achievement on each activity. This data collection is embedded in the activities because the journey log also serves Fifth Dimension purposes. The children are interested in keeping this record, so that they can figure out where they can go next and also so that their progress towards becoming a young wizard's assistant (YWA, or Wiz Kid) can be followed. (Children can become YWAs when they have reached high levels of performance on a specified number of the games and rooms of the maze.)

The maze structure also allows for embedded measurement by requiring children to engage in a wide variety of activities. Even if a child is primarily interested in playing arcade-type games, other kinds of games must be played as the child moves between the preferred games. This allows us to observe the child's level of mastery in several domains (for example, arithmetic, ecology, logic, spelling, reading, vocabulary, computer programming, history, or geography), as well as his or her skill in planning a route through the maze, while it also serves our hidden educational agenda of having the children participate in activities in a variety of domains.

For many of the skills of interest, we collect hard data by administering exam-like instruments appropriately embedded into an ongoing activity. Because the children are accustomed to using task cards that direct how they can play each game, the testing can be naturally integrated into the structured activity by placing the testing within the task card. Rather than taking a separate pretest before playing a particular game, the child just begins work on that game's task card which happens to begin by asking some questions. At one of our sites, both pretesting and posttesting of game-specific knowledge and skills is handled this way.

Control Groups. One of the thorniest problems we confront is control group definition and recruitment. The fundamental problem is that subjects self-select to participate in our program. Voluntary participation derives from our theoretical rationale and is a necessary component of our activity system; however, the one way in which the self-selection is not beneficial is that it makes the designation of a comparable control population very difficult. Evaluating the effects of Fifth Dimension participation on the children, of course, requires the ability to isolate those specific effects from effects resulting from other influences. Comparison of program participants with an otherwise comparable but nonparticipant control group is not the only way to measure a program's influence, but it is an especially strong method when it can be arranged.

The most methodologically sound approach to our control-group problem is the wait-list solution, in which half the children at a site who want to join the Fifth Dimension are randomly selected to participate immediately, and the other half are put on a waiting list to participate at a later date (after the data set has been collected). Because subjects are randomly assigned to the treatment and no-treatment conditions, the wait-list subjects form a true control group, and comparisons between those who have participated and those on the wait-list are completely justifiable. In this case, the only thing differentiating the controls from the participants is whether they have actually participated in the activity. Thus, measured differences between the groups must be due to some effect of the Fifth Dimension experience. Other potential influences on performance (such as maturation or school experiences) are equivalent for the two groups and, thus, can be isolated from Fifth Dimension effects on performance, avoiding many of the limitations of pre- and posttest designs.

Practical considerations have made it possible to have such true control groups at some sites. At our New Orleans site, for example, there are more children in the target population than can be handled at one time, so half of them get to be part of the Fifth Dimension in the fall, while the other half remain in the regular after-school setting and then join the Fifth Dimension for the spring. Comparison can thus be made at the end of the fall between groups that differ only in the variable of interest, that is, whether the children have participated in Fifth Dimension activity.

There are other methods available for getting reliable measurement, although they are less rigorous. Two of these methods in use among our sites are the recording of systematic preparticipation and postparticipation measurements, with the goal of assessing performance changes as a result of participation (this method includes various forms of control for the effects of repeated test administration) and the setting up of a matched, nonparticipant group on the basis of standardized test scores.

Game Performance Outcomes. The easiest and least intrusive measurement method is the simple recording of how well the child performs at each game or activity. Given our goal of embedding measurement into the ongoing activity, recording and evaluating game performance is a perfect measure. Since, as we described earlier, a child's performance level is recorded to determine the set of choices for the child's next activity, the necessary data collection is done for reasons intrinsic to the activity system.

For some of our games, the level of game achievement per se appears to have reasonable content validity. For example, children playing Botanical Gardens have to figure out what levels of light, temperature, soil richness, and water lead to greatest growth for a particular species of plant. On each trial, the child sets the level of each of these four variables and is then shown how tall the plant grew. The child performs many trials for a given plant, recording the conditions and the outcome for each trial, and he or she must perform the entire scientific reasoning task for several different plants in order to reach the level of expert as defined by the task card. If a child gets closer to the ideal answer for plants examined later in the game or gets to the ideal answer with fewer trials for those later plants, that is evidence in itself that the child is improving his or her mastery of the logic of experimentation as it is applied in the context of this game. Because the game itself so closely resembles the target skill, game performance per se can be seen as a measure of a relevant specific skill or body of knowledge. Other games for which this is true involve manipulating fractions, using geographical information, classifying relationships among pairs of words, and using combinatorics. Through many different ways of measuring game outcomes, we do find that the children improve their performance with practice. Thus, our data show that Fifth Dimension activity has a positive effect on the children's skill or knowledge in many domains with academic relevance.

However, there is still the question of what cognitive structures the child has appropriated beyond the actual game. For games whose relationships to the skills and knowledge we are most interested in is less obvious or less direct than in the examples above, the issue is even more pressing. What distance of transfer do we expect, or should we expect? For example, when a child becomes an expert in the game of Artillery, accurately setting the angle of the cannon and the amount of powder to use to blow up the enemy fort over the hill, how much knowledge of geometry and/or physics has the child gained beyond the specific requirements of the game (Newman, Griffin, and Cole, 1989)?

These questions of validity have required us to be careful in interpreting the observation that children generally get better at Fifth Dimension games with practice. How far does a skill transfer need to go in order to provide convincing evidence of improvement in school-relevant skills? Can anyone expect to find measurable changes in global aspects of school performance from an activity that a child does for a few hours a week for half a year? Game performance in itself is not adequate to address these questions, so we have had to employ the alternative methods that are discussed next.

Skills and Knowledge Assessment. Our assessment work has been substantially focused on developing good measures of the skills and knowledge relevant to Fifth Dimension activity, with minimal intrusion into the children's ongoing activity. This has been simpler for some skills than others. For example, because writing is a focal activity, we have worked on refining several measures of the children's writing competency. These measures include the use (or adaptation) of standardized tests such as the Test of Written Language-2 (TOWL) by two of our sites (King and McNamee, 1992) and the development of our own scoring and analysis systems for the children's letters and stories, in order to explore aspects of the children's writing that are somewhat specific to our program (for example, the use of conventional letter formats, the number of topics included in each letter, and the inclusion of personal information). By the TOWL measure used at two sites, there was no reliable gain in writing performance over an eight-month interval of participation in the Fifth Dimension. Other, more qualitative analyses showed promising, but not definitive, changes over time in letter topics chosen and word-processing features used, such as varied fonts and character formats.

Since we have multiple sources of information on each child, gathered over a period of weeks and months, we have excellent data for case study approaches to measuring the development of writing skills. One example of the use of this method is a case study that was performed at our Chicago site and that showed progress in one child's story-writing skills over the course of several weeks (King and McNamee, 1992).

Another focal area is the development of children's computer literacy, including their comfort and familiarity with technology. We have developed a computer-literacy instrument, administered at several sites, specifically testing children's knowledge of such things as the parts of the computer, their functions, and the procedures for turning computers on and off, using diskettes, using a mouse, and doing word processing. Using this test, we found significant improvement between pre- and posttest scores for children at the San Marcos site (Schustack and Worden, 1993). The children especially showed improvement on the portion of the test relevant to word processing on the Macintosh (a central activity at that site). Children at the New Orleans site who took an adapted version of the test (altered to reflect the machines and activities at that site) also showed significant improvement.

The daily field notes of the wizard's assistants are another source of data for many evaluation questions of interest to us. In these notes, the assistants give fairly detailed recollections of the specific interactions and activities they participated in or witnessed each day. These notes thus document the social construction of knowledge from the adults' perspectives, illustrating the learning-scaffold building process that takes place when experts and novices intersubjectively experience an engaging activity. The field notes yield information about the children's social interactions, their strategies, and the ideas and reactions that they communicate to the wizard's assistants with whom they work and play. One site has put its field notes into a computer data base, which can be systematically probed for various information, allowing the selection of all passages that refer to a particular child, a specific activity, or any keyword (or phrase or set of keywords or phrases) relevant to a question of interest. This field notes data base has been used for a case study on strategies in a particular game as these strategies evolved over the course of one child's joint activity with an adult (Laboratory of Comparative Human Cognition, 1993).

Issues of language proficiency and language change among bilingual children are addressed at the Spanish-English bilingual sites, where the Language Assessment Scales (LAS) have documented changes in the children's reading, writing, listening, and speaking in both languages. At the Michigan La Clase Mágica site, participating children have shown improvement relative to nonparticipant control children on the English reading and writing subtests of the LAS instrument. At the Solana Beach La Clase Mágica site, participating children showed more improvement than the control group on both English and Spanish portions of the test (Vásquez, 1993).

Relation to Learning Within School Settings

Many focal areas in our program are related to the knowledge and skills taught in traditional schools. We have a strong focus on the basic skills of reading, writing, and mathematics, as well as on geography and science. There is overlap with school learning in some of the content of the instructional play materials as well. Many of the children at our sites play some of the same computer games in their schools that they can play in the Fifth Dimension (for example: Oregon Trail for social studies, Where in the World Is Carmen San Diego? for geography, and MathBlasters for arithmetic). What is vastly different from the schools' practices is our approach. We focus not on teaching but on facilitating learning. In the Fifth Dimension environment, adults tend to work as collaborative partners with the children, engaged in activities in which both can learn. We encourage individual exploration on a self-paced schedule. We support the children's becoming more self-motivated. We encourage peer collaboration and extensive adult contact with children individually or in small groups. The adult-to-child ratio in the Fifth Dimension room at some sites is close to 1:2, a vast difference from the ratios the children experience in their public and parochial school classrooms.

Evolving Research Collaborations

We have experienced many changes resulting from interactions among the collaborators on this project. Individually and as a group, we have dynamic, growing, and changing agendas. This chapter has focused primarily on the first two years of implementing and developing research sites in a multiyear project. Change in personnel, activities, site locations, and evaluation methods has become an integral part of the overall project. Some changes have resulted from our sharing, within our research consortium, of successful new techniques and approaches both in running our sites and in evaluating the program's effects.

At the start of this project, the six primary consortium sites were paired into three partnerships on the basis of research interests and populations: one partnership focused on issues of instruction, development, and computer literacy; a second focused on issues of bilingualism in speaking and writing among Latino youngsters; and the third focused on ways to improve the literacy of African American youngsters through writing and play. While these initial pairings continue to play some role in our interactions, we have found that other pairs and triads have evolved. Our overlapping research interests have been enhanced by the variety of methodologies, populations, and environments that each site provides. In particular, our collaborations have been enhanced as each member of the consortium encounters specific examples of the usefulness of previously unfamiliar methodologies from other disciplines, applied in research settings focused on questions similar to our own.

Consortium members collaborate largely via electronic mail in a frequent and open conversation, with the whole consortium receiving copies of most messages. Teleconferencing also gives us a simple way to interact with colleagues in other locales when our interactions with these colleagues via formal reports, regular mail, or attendance at scientific meetings occur too infrequently to be of ongoing value in pursuing joint research. Thus, the overriding research agenda is largely pursued in a distributed, electronic virtual community that mirrors the Fifth Dimension's extended after-school "virtual culture of collaborative learning" (Nicolopoulou and Cole, in press). Fifth Dimension activity binds together children, university students and other adults, host institutions and universities, and our research consortium in an unusual and mutually positive endeavor. Our goals of enhancing children's literacy skills, collaborative skills, and technological literacy are pursued in ways that themselves rely on communication, collaboration, and technology.

References

Carnegie Council on Adolescent Development. *A Matter of Time: Risk and Opportunity in the Nonschool Hours.* Report of the Task Force on Youth Development and Community Programs. Washington, D.C.: Carnegie Council on Adolescent Development, 1992.

Dewey, J. *Democracy and Education.* New York: Macmillan, 1916.

Engestrom, Y., and Punamiki, R. *Activity Theory.* New York: Cambridge University Press, 1993.

Griffin, P., and Cole, M. "Current Activity for the Future: The Zo-ped." In B. Rogoff and J. V. Wertsch (eds.), *Children's Learning in the "Zone of Proximal Development."* San Francisco: Jossey-Bass, 1984.

King, C., and McNamee, G. "The Development of Children's Voices in Written Language in Their Home Communities and in Far Away Places." Paper presented at the Conference for Sociocultural Research, Madrid, Spain, 1992.

Laboratory of Comparative Human Cognition, University of California, San Diego. "An Assessment of Learning Through the Qualitative Analysis of Fieldnotes." Paper presented at the Conference on Assessment and Diversity, Santa Cruz, Calif., Feb. 1993.

Luria, A. R. *The Making of Mind: A Personal Account of Soviet Psychology.* (M. Cole and S. Cole, eds.) Cambridge, Mass.: Harvard University Press, 1979.

Newman, D., Griffin, P., and Cole, M. *The Construction Zone: Working for Cognitive Change in School.* New York: Cambridge University Press, 1989.

Nicolopoulou, A., and Cole, M. "The Generation and Transmission of Shared Knowledge in the Culture of Collaborative Learning: The Fifth Dimension, Its Play-World, and Its Institutional Contexts." In E. A. Forman, N. Minick, and C. A. Stone (eds.), *Contexts for Learning: Sociocultural Dynamics in Children's Development.* New York: Oxford University Press, in press.

Rogoff, B., and Wertsch, J. V. (eds.). *Children's Learning in the "Zone of Proximal Development."* San Francisco: Jossey-Bass, 1984.

Schustack, M. W., and Worden, P. E. "Assessing the Impact of Afterschool Activity on Children's Computer Knowledge." Unpublished manuscript, California State University, San Marcos, 1993.

Vásquez, O.A. "A Look at Language as a Resource: Lesson from La Clase Mágica." In National Society for the Study of Education, *Bilingual Education.* Chicago: University of Chicago Press, 1993.

Vygotsky, L. S. *Mind in Society: The Development of Higher Psychological Processes.* (M. Cole, V. John-Steiner, S. Scribner, and E. Souberman, eds.) Cambridge, Mass.: Harvard University Press, 1978.

MIRIAM W. SCHUSTACK is assistant professor of psychology at California State University, San Marcos.

CATHERINE KING is assistant professor of psychology at Elon College in North Carolina.

MARGARET A. GALLEGO is assistant professor of teacher education at Michigan State University.

OLGA A. VÁSQUEZ is assistant professor of communication and is affiliated with the Laboratory of Comparative Human Cognition at the University of California, San Diego.

This chapter describes a self-directed after-school program that is based on equal participation and input from youths, teachers, and researchers.

On the Edge of School: Creating a New Context for Students' Development

*Thomas Hatch, Heidi Goodrich,
Christopher Unger, Gwynne H. Wiatrowski*

Three years ago, in the basement of the Mather Elementary School in Dorchester, Massachusetts, a group of third-, fourth-, and fifth-grade after-school students gathered to watch a video about a circus. The activity was intended to inspire the students to think about what kind of circus performer they might like to portray in a variety show they were producing. But when the teacher passed out pencils and paper so that the students could describe their characters, one student looked at the materials and said, "What's this for? We're not supposed to do any work in here." The teacher and a researcher who were present had assumed that the context was appropriate for a writing activity. Clearly, for this student, the after-school setting had an entirely different purpose. Two years later, however, students' perceptions of the Mather Afterschool Project had changed. For example, when two students approached one of the program directors and asked if they could have some money to go on a field trip to a nearby pizzeria, the director asked them to write a proposal that explained where they wanted to go, how much it would cost, and why they should be allowed to go. The students turned around, went back to their classroom, and wrote a proposal. For them, this writing

This chapter is an early report from a collaborative research program supported in part by Pew Charitable Trusts, the MacArthur Foundation, the Spencer Foundation, and Freedom House through a grant from New England Telephone. The principal investigators for this project are William Damon, Howard Gardner, and David Perkins. The data presented and statements made are solely the responsibility of the authors. We thank Allan Collins, Joyce Conkling, Carol Gignoux, Dominique Gilmer, Michael K. Marshall, Sabine Pierre-Jules, Uyen Chi Nguyen, Traci Turner, and the editors of this volume.

activity was not out of context; it was a natural part of what they did in the after-school program.

Often, when an individual's behavior changes, the tendency is to credit or blame that individual. In this instance, however, it was not simply the students who had improved their skills, attitudes, and approach to work. Over the two years, the context had changed. Even though its location has not moved, the after-school program is now a different place. This chapter describes the program and its goals, and then traces the program's evolution as a context for learning over the past three years. In the process, three critical aspects of this evolution are discussed. First, the after-school projects have changed and become more engaging for students and easier for teachers to use. Second, the students, teachers, and researchers have developed common goals and expectations. Third, the teachers and researchers have learned how to share their knowledge and responsibilities. Each of these factors has contributed to the achievement of a new after-school culture—including assumptions and patterns of behavior—that reinforces project-based activities and self-directed learning. As a result, program participants are carrying out activities in which their predecessors could not or did not want to be engaged during the first year. In conclusion, the chapter draws some general lessons for the creation of other contexts for learning both in and out of school.

Background and Goals

The Mather Afterschool Project was developed as a collaboration between psychologists William Damon, Howard Gardner, David Perkins, and Allan Collins and Mather School principal Michael K. Marshall. The Mather School is a public elementary school located in a culturally diverse urban neighborhood in Boston. Seventy-six percent of the school's 640 students receive free or reduced price meals, more than half live with a single parent, and over a third come from homes where English is not spoken. Forty-five third, fourth, and fifth graders from the school attend the after-school program for one hour and forty-five minutes four days a week. Many of the after-school students have poor academic records or trouble interacting with others. They are selected from a pool of applicants by the after-school teaching staff, and each year, about fifteen students from the previous year's program return.

The program is run by six Mather School teachers with the help of four members of the research staff. Each teacher works with a group of fifteen students two days a week, and the teachers are paid for their participation. Three teachers have been with the program for three years, two stayed for two years, and five spent no more than one year in the program. Teachers' primary reasons for leaving the program were other responsibilities (primarily child care) and moving to jobs in other schools. Currently, each teacher leads his or her group in one of six projects twice a week. These projects last about eight to ten weeks and include such pursuits as publishing a newspaper, designing board games, and organizing a recycling drive. Over the course of the year, each group participates in all six projects.

The researchers' participation in this effort was based on a series of hypotheses about project-based instruction and about the difficulty of creating innovative approaches within traditional educational institutions. Projects involve the pursuit of a specific goal over an extended period of time, and ultimately, project activity should yield a product, performance, or event (Blumenfeld and others, in press; Katz and Chard, 1989; Veenema, Meyaard, and Walters, 1991). In contrast to worksheets and other conventional classroom exercises, projects are assumed to be engaging because they have a meaningful connection to life and work outside of school. Therefore, the researchers took as one of their two primary goals the development of a project-based approach that would provide a supportive context for the development of a variety of skills. In particular, they hoped that projects would give students opportunities for using literacy skills (for example, by writing articles) and for using thinking skills (for example, by analyzing the forms and functions of different objects or the costs and benefits of different choices). In addition, the researchers anticipated that experience with projects would allow students to develop such characteristics of self-directed learners as remaining focused for long periods of time, persisting in a line of inquiry, considering multiple options, and revising one's work. The researchers also hypothesized that student learning would be increased if the projects were accompanied by a variety of teaching strategies: coaching—in which teachers model appropriate activities and facilitate rather than direct the students' work—fostering peer collaboration, and employing alternative assessments (Collins, Brown, and Holum, 1991; Collins, Brown, and Newman, 1989; Damon, 1984; Damon and Phelps, 1989, 1990; Gardner, 1992).

The other major goal of the program was to develop methods that would support the introduction of projects as a widespread means of instruction. Despite the promise of projects, developing and sustaining such an innovative approach within the institutional constraints of the regular school day is difficult (Cremin, 1961; Cuban, 1984; Graham, 1967). Projects represent a departure from the educational practices and goals with which many teachers are most familiar and feel most comfortable. The institutional pressures of tests, grades, and other school demands discourage teachers from developing or implementing projects that take more than a single period to complete; similarly, the demands of writing newspaper articles or running a business go far beyond much of the work that is required in many schools. Therefore, it was hypothesized that an after-school program, free from the institutional constraints of school, would be a more supportive context for the development of project methods than would a regular classroom.

As the program has evolved over the last three years, the teachers and researchers have used a variety of qualitative methods to investigate these hypotheses and document the program's progress. These methods include observing in the after-school program, interviewing both teachers and students, and collecting students' after-school work. In addition, during the third year of the program, data were collected from both after-school students and a control group of their peers on several quantitative measures and these data are currently being analyzed.

First Year

During the first year of the program, 1990-1991, the two primary goals were pursued through two long-term projects. One was a drama project for which the students spent a portion of the year producing a variety show featuring skits and songs. In the process, the students were involved in doing acting exercises, writing scripts, building sets, designing costumes, and carrying out other activities related to the final performance. They spent the rest of their time in a design project for which they designed and built bridges, flying objects, and other constructions. Planning of the projects took place largely during monthly meetings among the teachers and the research team and in occasional small-group meetings. Most activities were directed by the teachers, but the research staff took primary responsibility for developing and piloting several activities within the design project.

Recognizing the Need for Collaboration. Almost from the beginning, it was clear that the after-school setting was not as conducive to the development and piloting of an innovative educational approach as the researchers had predicted. The removal of the pressures of tests and grades did give the teachers more freedom to experiment with new curricula. At the same time, however, the after-school context supported teacher aims and expectations that were not entirely consistent with those of the research team. In interviews and meetings throughout the year, the teachers revealed that they did not view the development of literacy skills as the primary goal of an after-school setting. For the most part, they believed an after-school program was most appropriate for the development of student self-esteem and the building of healthy relationships: activities critical to the long-term happiness and success of the students and often neglected during the regular school day. One teacher explained at the end of the first year, "I wanted to build [the students'] self-esteem. I wanted them to get a clearer idea of who they are and what their talents are and what they can achieve, to give them more fuel to go into their classrooms every day, feel better about themselves, and therefore, do better work. So I would have to say that self-esteem building and unraveling the mysteries of who they are to them . . . those were my goals." Similar statements were repeated throughout the researchers' interviews with the other teachers.

In addition, working in an after-school program at the end of a long school day placed serious limits on the time and attention the teachers could devote to developing a new educational approach. They found it more efficient—and often more successful—to engage the students in recreational activities like board games and outdoor play than to try to carry out literacy or thinking skills activities that they as teachers had never attempted before. While, for the most part, teachers and researchers got along well, the different expectations and the teachers' working conditions made collaboration more difficult than the researchers had expected.

Uncovering Students' Point of View. The students' attitudes and behavior were also affected by the after-school context. In year-end interviews, the students revealed that they had never perceived the after-school program as the engaging place that either the researchers or teachers had intended. For example, the student in the following interview focused on a negative, school-related reason for his participation in the program.

SAM: I told [my friends] it was fun down here.
INTERVIEWER: So how come they didn't come?
SAM: Because they don't do nothing to get in trouble so they can come down here, or do nothing bad.
INTERVIEWER: Say that again?
SAM: I said, they don't do nothing crazy like or just something bad.
INTERVIEWER: That's how you get in here?
SAM: Yeah, I act crazy, so I'm being counseled, getting tutored, and I'm down here.
INTERVIEWER: So you think you're down here because you were bad?
SAM: Probably.
INTERVIEWER: Is everybody down here because they were bad?
SAM: No.
INTERVIEWER: How come kids are down here?
SAM: It's probably because of the work. Because we do some work, right? And some of us got F's.

Despite the fact that the program was supposed to take place outside the context of school, the students seemed to view it in terms of their experiences during the regular school day, that is, as another in a long line of remedial activities.

The students' lack of experience with project-based activities during the regular school day also presented a special challenge. In conventional curricula, where teachers control activities or students carry out explicit instructions for relatively short periods of time, students have little need to take charge of their own activities. To perform projects, however, students have to be considerably more self-directed. During the first year of the program, observations showed that, even after a project was explained to them, students would often ask what they should do and relied on the teachers to guide them through the activities. Thus, while the projects were intended to give students experience in directing their own activities, many neither expected nor knew how to take advantage of this opportunity.

These first year experiences suggested that moving outside the school curriculum and schedule does not necessarily mean that institutional pressures can be left behind. In this case, teachers, students, and researchers all brought to the program expectations about what should (and should not) happen after school and these expectations were based on their previous classroom experiences. In addition, the time and energy that both students and teachers were required to invest in the regular school day affected what they were able and willing to do after school.

Second Year

After the first year, it was clear that simply carrying out projects in an after-school setting was not enough to help students develop expectations and skills that are not traditionally emphasized in schools. In order to create a more supportive context, both researchers and teachers felt the projects needed to be simplified. To make the projects easier to implement, the research staff decided to share some of the practical and organizational responsibilities by acting as "co-teachers" in the program. In addition, both teachers and researchers tried to create a common expectation among all participants that the after-school program was a place where students would learn literacy and thinking skills. The hope was that the changes in the way the projects were designed, the work was distributed, and the program was viewed would create conditions more supportive of project-based learning.

Revising the Projects. In the second year, the teachers and researchers created six projects that lasted about eight to ten weeks each. Teachers and researchers discussed these projects together during the summer, but the researchers took on the primary responsibility for writing up curriculum guides. These guides included detailed scripts, which delineated the steps to go through and even the questions to ask and which were intended to make it easier for teachers to meet the goals the research team endorsed. For example, in the flight project, teachers were given step-by-step instructions that explained how to help students learn such thinking skills as comparison and contrast and the analysis of form and function while the students built home-made flying objects. These scripts also explained how to use the three teaching strategies mentioned earlier of coaching, fostering peer collaboration, and employing alternative assessments. For example, the instructions detailed how the teachers should coach the students by modeling the use of thinking skills in a discussion of a flight test of a paper airplane.

While the students found these new projects much more engaging than the previous ones, it was hard for the teachers to follow the curriculum scripts. With little time to prepare for the activities after the end of the regular school day, teachers needed to refer constantly to the instructions in order to know what to do. Although following the scripts ensured that the three teaching strategies would be used, this rigid procedure interfered with the teachers' ability to take advantage of the unanticipated and spontaneous interests of the students. As a consequence, some of the projects had no more meaning for the students than conventional classroom exercises. In other words, the way the projects were constructed and written up created conditions that conflicted with one of the basic goals of a project-based curriculum.

Creating Collaboration. At the beginning of the second year, it quickly became clear that it was unrealistic to expect teachers in an after-school setting to carry out the kinds of detailed projects that had been designed. As one teacher explained, "It's hard to take the after-school program plus your full day if you're a school teacher and to juggle those. . . . It's a lot of work. It's not just, oh, we come down there, they have free time, and then that's it. It's like a lesson you have to teach and maybe in different forms than you do during the school day."

It was in order to respond to this concern that the researchers changed their roles just a few weeks into the fall term, and instead of acting simply as observers, became co-teachers; they took on and shared responsibilities for working with the students and for carrying out the projects. As a result, each teacher was accompanied by a researcher at least once a week in the after-school program. This shift created considerable time for teachers and researchers to work together. Researchers could consult with the teachers about the direction of the projects as they unfolded. Instead of waiting for a separate teacher-researcher meeting before reflecting on what could have been done during the activities, researchers and teachers were able to pool their expertise and make changes and adjustments on the spot. Further, the researchers were able to share some of the practical problems of implementation and to model the use of the teaching strategies with which teachers were unfamiliar or uncomfortable. In addition to this shift in the researchers' roles, teachers and researchers also established regular biweekly meetings so they could reflect on the progress of the projects as a group.

These changes in the project approach and in the relationship between the teachers and researchers contributed to an unexpected result. When asked to describe what they had learned in the after-school program during the second year, the teachers were almost unanimous in suggesting that the program helped them learn how to think on their feet and how to adapt their lesson plans to events going on in the classroom. One teacher described,

> I've planned . . . [that] it should be a full hour project in the classroom, and it turns out to be ten, fifteen minutes. What do I do now? I think this after-school program gives you that filler: what you can do [in this situation], how to expand on a project. . . . You have to think on your feet all the time down there. . . . It's like an extension. It's what do you do after you write the story? What do you do in the middle to fill in, to make the story better and make it fun, so it's not a task?

Thus, the teachers were gaining both the skills and the support that they needed in order to make projects into substantive and engaging learning activities. In addition, close collaboration gave the teachers and researchers a chance to develop a common understanding of both the problems and the possibilities of projects.

Changing Students' Expectations. While the shift in roles gave the teachers and researchers a chance to share their ideas and goals, a change in the selection procedure for the second year helped shape students' perceptions of the program and the projects. In the first year, Mather School teachers had been asked to identify their most "at-risk" students (those most likely to be retained at the end of the year or to cause problems in the classroom), and then forty-two of these students had been "invited" to the program. In the second year, the goals of the program—including the expectations that students would be writing and thinking—were explained, the projects were described, and interested students were asked to apply. One hundred and twenty students completed the application, and out of this applicant pool, a group of forty-five students was selected. The selected group represented the range of the school population but still emphasized students who were experiencing social or academic difficulties. As a result, students who joined the after-school activity did not feel that it was a remedial program. In fact, the attendance figures, observations, and interviews demonstrated that the students were much more engaged in the projects and the program than they had been in the first year. Like many after-school programs, the Mather program suffered attendance problems during its first year. In the three different groups of fourteen students each, average daily attendance was about five students. During the second year, however, there was a dramatic improvement. Table 5.1 shows first- and second-year average attendance patterns in April and May, the only months for which first-year data are available but also the months when dropout rates and truancy tend to be highest.

Changes in the students' approach to the projects were also evident to their teachers. The four after-school teachers who worked in both the first and second years reported that, compared to first-year students, second-year students were more active, independent, and persistent and sustained their interest longer. A teacher who saw a change in a student who had been unwilling to become involved in almost any activity at the beginning of the year reported,

> He reminded me of this big rock that I could never move and put in the right place because he was so heavy. And I just remember always, physically, I'd be tired from trying to move [him] around the room. . . . But when we started working on the project, about halfway through, he started participating without having to be moved physically or coaxed. . . . And I also noticed that he would come to me for help, which he wasn't doing before. And he would ask for things. And he would sit down and do his work and suddenly he stopped being that immovable rock.

Table 5.1. Attendance Data for April and May of the Mather Afterschool Project's First Two Years

	Average Number Attending Daily		Number Attending at Least 75% of Days	
	First Year (1990–1991)	Second Year (1991–1992)	First Year (1990-1991)	Second Year (1991-1992)
Group 1	4.4	9.7	3	9
Group 2	6.2	10.8	3	11
Group 3	5.9	9.7	3	9

Taken together, teachers' observations and interviews suggested that the after-school setting was becoming a different place for students than it had been during the first year. It was becoming a place where students viewed literacy activities differently than they did in school, and a place where the students wanted and were able to be involved in projects that required them to be self-directed.

Third Year

After the second year, both the teachers and researchers felt that, together, they had created some of the conditions needed to support project-based learning: the students, teachers, and researchers had common expectations about the program, organizational responsibilities were taken care of, and the projects themselves were engaging. At the same time, the projects were still difficult for the teachers to implement on their own. In addition, there was still relatively little connection between what the students and teachers did from one project to the next. As a result, some projects were much more successful than others, and everyone involved felt the students were not gaining as much from the after-school experience as they could. In order to address these issues, teachers and researchers identified the critical features of the most successful projects; they also sought to create a series of related learning experiences across the projects; and then teachers took on even greater responsibility for developing and directing the projects than they had the year before.

Giving Teachers Project Ownership. During the summer before the program's third year, the teachers and researchers continued to develop a collaborative relationship by holding a series of meetings in order to reflect on the progress of the program. At these meetings, they identified the development of more specific and consistent learning goals across the projects as a primary program need. They decided to focus on three skills: writing, reflecting, and solving design problems (such as those found in designing a cookbook or a newsletter, for example).

In addition to developing these specific goals, they also substantially changed the way they created and produced the projects. They still created a variety of eight- to ten-week projects: students were to publish a newspaper, organize and go on field trips of their own choice, design board games, prepare healthy snacks, and develop their own responses to social and environmental problems like violence and pollution. But instead of generating detailed scripts in advance, the teachers and researchers created general curriculum guidelines and optional activities. This approach enabled the teachers to mold the projects around the students' interest as well as to use the three teaching strategies when the appropriate occasions arose.

Through their increased participation in developing the goals for the year and in selecting and developing the projects, the teachers gained a sense of ownership of the projects. They no longer felt as if they had to adhere to someone else's script, and without such detailed instructions, they were in a better position to carry out the projects. This sense of ownership set the stage for the teachers to take the lead in project implementation. As a result, by the end of the third year, four teachers who had been with the program for at least two years were carrying out their projects largely without the support of the research staff. While one of the two new teachers left the program for personal reasons, the other took the initiative in redesigning her project after the Christmas vacation. Making such changes was something the program veterans had not been comfortable doing until their second year. One veteran teacher went as far as to exclaim that she "had" her project now; after experimenting with a variety of different projects for three years, she felt that she now knew what she needed to do. She is currently planning to carry out the same project during the fourth year.

Emerging Project Framework. The teachers and researchers continued their joint reflections about the projects in biweekly meetings throughout the third year. During the meetings, the most successful projects were reviewed and four common features were identified (Goodrich, Hatch, Wiatrowski, and Unger, n.d.). They found that the most successful projects were genuine, provided natural reasons for students to use literacy and thinking skills, had clear goals and steps, and offered a number of options. These features are discussed in detail in the rest of this section.

First, the most successful projects were of genuine interest to both the teacher and students. Projects that had a real outcome or a public product, like the organization and taking of a field trip and the publication or distribution of a newspaper, provided meaningful goals that both students and teachers wanted to achieve. Projects like the building and testing of flying objects were ones that did not have meaningful goals for the students and were less likely to keep students engaged for long periods of time. Second, the most successful projects also contained natural reasons for students to use literacy or thinking skills. The newspaper project gave students a reason to write that made sense to them; similarly, the field trip project gave students a practical reason to use comparison and contrast and to think about the pros and cons of each alternative in order to select a field trip that both fit a specific budget and the interests of their peers.

Third, projects also seemed to work most smoothly when the steps to a goal were clear to both teachers and students: in order to publish a newspaper, articles had to be written, laid out, and printed; in order to go on a field trip, possibilities had to be identified, costs considered, options debated, and decisions made. Finally, the most effective projects still had considerable flexibility even though the basic steps were clear. This flexibility made it possible for teachers to take advantage of students' interests and ideas as they arose. For the newspaper project, students could carry out interviews, review books or movies, write about themselves, or create cartoons or other artwork; for the field trip project, students could choose from a wide range of possible trips. In this manner, the projects provided the inspiration, support, and freedom that the students needed to work independently and in a self-directed manner.

The changes made as the program progressed contributed to a marked increase in students' involvement in substantive literacy activities and in students' productivity. This increase was most evident in the amount and variety of student writing. For example, in the first year, student writing was largely confined to autobiographies and some scripts for skits. In the second year, students primarily wrote newspaper articles and scripts for public service announcements. In the third year, however, students wrote articles, proposals describing why they wanted to go on particular field trips or make certain recipes, step-by-step instructions to accompany jewelry and games they made, and letters, rap songs, and skits that addressed issues like violence and homelessness. As one teacher explained, "I found kids who would do more than one [article] or work together to write a really long story, and they would go back at it and change things and look at their writing and analyze it and decide whether or not [it was good]." Data from a pre- and posttest are currently being analyzed in order to determine whether or not there were statistically significant increases in the quality of the students' writing over the course of the third year.

As in the second year, teachers in the third year noted that as the students worked on the projects they became much more independent and self-directed. In explaining her goals for the program, one teacher described the changes in the students from their first to their third project this way:

> I think my goals [for them] were exactly what they did—to be independent and their own [boss], to set their goals, to decide what their purpose is and go for it. . . . 'Cause the first time [they did a project], they're looking like, "what do we have to do?" . . . That always gets me going: "Okay, so you're looking for me. You want me to tell you what to do?" The third time around, I didn't get "what do you want me to do?" [They would say,] "I'm doing [this]." . . . They knew what they were doing.

The teachers' impressions of improved student participation were consistent with the weekly observations carried out by the research staff. Videotaped observations from the third year are currently being analyzed in order to confirm these findings and to compare the behavior of new after-school students to those who have been in the program for a year or more.

Conclusion

The teachers' and researchers' experience with the Mather Afterschool Project shows that the act of shifting institutional constraints was far from sufficient to support the introduction of innovative curricula. Even though it lacked the pressures of tests, grades, and other school demands, the program was still influenced by teachers', researchers', and students' existing beliefs and patterns of behavior that made it difficult for all involved to develop and carry out successful projects. This finding suggests that researchers and others interested in stimulating educational reforms need to pay particular attention to several critical factors in order to develop contexts and cultures that support nonconventional learning experiences.

First of all, creating a context for learning means creating common expectations among the participants. Even in this case, where participants volunteered for the program and endorsed the initiative, it took considerable time to produce common understandings and shared goals. Simply agreeing on or adopting goals or standards is not sufficient. In the absence of a deep and shared understanding of goals, new skills and behaviors that promote those goals are unlikely to be recognized or rewarded. Second, regardless of participants' assumptions, practical constraints need to be identified and addressed. Too often, teachers and others are expected to create new programs through sheer force of will, by working overtime and/or on multiple initiatives at once. Whether through the support of other people who can take on some of the burden temporarily, or by compensating for increased demands in other ways, researchers and reformers have to take seriously the work that surrounds the task of facilitating learning and not just the learning itself.

Third, the work carried out in an educational setting must be free to evolve along with the goals of the participants and the demands of the practical constraints. In this case, if the researchers had clung to their idea of what project-based learning and an after-school program should look like, it would have been extremely difficult for researchers, teachers, and students to develop common goals and expectations or to develop a sense of personal ownership and investment in the program. In addition, the work with teachers would have remained focused on the three teaching strategies and the additional characteristics of successful projects that were defined along the way would never have emerged. While a closer adherence to the researchers' initial ideas might have made it possible to test those ideas more faithfully, the teachers and researchers would have been unable to create the kind of culture that could support a successful program outcome.

Finally, the teachers and researchers have tried to incorporate these lessons into materials and workshops that are currently being developed about the project approach. Rather than prepare a book of projects for teachers or after-school programs to implement, they are developing guidelines that are intended to help others create their own projects. In addition to these guidelines, the teachers and researchers are continuing to document the strategies that make projects particularly effective educational experiences, and they are compiling information on specific classroom routines that can minimize the practical difficulties of instituting projects in different settings. It is their hope that by bringing these ideas together, they can contribute to the transformation of more than the classroom curriculum and support the development of new contexts and cultures for learning. Through these ideas, they hope to gain insights into how the development of individuals can be yoked to the development of the learning context itself.

References

Blumenfeld, P., Soloway, E., Marx, R., Krajcik, J., Guzdial, M., and Palincsar, A. "Motivating Project-Based Learning." *Educational Psychologist*, in press.

Collins, A., Brown, J. S., and Holum, A. "Cognitive Apprenticeship: Making Thinking Visible." *American Educator*, 1991, *15* (3), 6–11.

Collins, A., Brown, J. S., and Newman, S. E. "Cognitive Apprenticeship: Teaching the Crafts of Reading, Writing, and Mathematics." In L. B. Resnick (ed.), *Knowing, Learning and Instruction: Essays in Honor of Robert Glaser*. Hillsdale, N.J.: Erlbaum, 1989.

Cremin, L. *The Transformation of the School: Progressivism in American Education, 1876–1957.* New York: Vintage Books, 1961.

Cuban, L. *How Teachers Taught: Constancy and Change in American Classrooms, 1890–1980.* New York: Longman, 1984.

Damon, W. "Peer Education: The Untapped Potential." *Journal of Applied Developmental Psychology*, 1984, *5*, 331–343.

Damon, W., and Phelps, E. "Strategic Uses of Peer Learning in Children's Education." In T. Berndt and G. Ladd (eds.), *Peer Relationships in Child Development*. New York: Wiley, 1989.

Damon, W., and Phelps, E. "Critical Distinctions Among Three Approaches to Peer Education. *International Journal of Educational Research*, 1990, *13* (1), 9–19.

Gardner, H. "Assessment in Context: The Alternative to Standardized Testing." In B. Gifford and M. O'Connor (eds.), *Changing Assessments: Alternative Views of Aptitude, Achievement, and Instruction*. Boston: Kluwer, 1992.

Goodrich, H., Hatch, T., Wiatrowski, G., and Unger, C. *A Guide to Developing Projects.* Cambridge, Mass.: Project Zero, Harvard Graduate School of Education, n.d.

Graham, P. *Progressive Education from Arcady to Academe: A History of the Progressive Education Association.* New York: Teachers College Press, 1967.

Katz, L., and Chard, S. *Engaging Children's Minds: The Project Approach.* Norwood, N.J.: Ablex Publishing, 1989.

Veenema, S., Meyaard, J., and Walters, J. *Projects and Computers. (Technical Report.)* Cambridge, Mass.: Project Zero, Harvard Graduate School of Education, 1991.

THOMAS HATCH *is a research associate at Project Zero, Harvard Graduate School of Education, and director of the ATLAS Seminar.*

HEIDI GOODRICH *is a doctoral student at Harvard Graduate School of Education and a research assistant at Project Zero.*

CHRISTOPHER UNGER *is a research associate at Project Zero and adjunct faculty at Lesley College in Cambridge, Massachusetts.*

GWYNNE H. WIATROWSKI *is a research assistant at Project Zero, Harvard Graduate School of Education.*

This chapter describes the nature of Mexican American and European American parents' aspirations for their children's futures and the links between family resources and community resources.

Aspirations of Low-Income Mexican American and European American Parents for Their Children and Adolescents

Catherine R. Cooper, Margarita Azmitia,
Eugene E. Garcia, Angela Ittel, Edward Lopez,
Lourdes Rivera, Rebeca Martínez-Chávez

Among the settings of children's learning and development outside of school, families are considered a central context for children's mastery of important cultural tools. Contemporary analyses emphasize the "cultural capital" or "funds of knowledge" that parents pass on to their children (Mehan, 1992; Moll, Velez-Ibanez, and Gonzalez, 1991), but Harkness, Super, and Keefer (1992) also note that "theories of culture acquisition must deal with the reality of cultural change" (p. 163). In this chapter, we consider the accommodations that parents make when they immigrate to a new culture or move into a new ecological niche within their present culture. In particular, we exam-

The work reported in this chapter was made possible by grants from the Office of Educational Research and Improvement, U.S. Department of Education and from the Bilingual Research Group and the Social Sciences Division of the University of California, Santa Cruz. The support of the National Center for Research in Cultural Diversity and Second Language Learning at the University of California, Santa Cruz is gratefully acknowledged. In addition, we thank Jack Mallory, Marisa Amin, Nancy Blonston, Marcela Lopez, Deanne Perez, Patricia Reilly, Anthony Villar, Robert G. Cooper, Barbara Rogoff, the principals and teachers of the Watsonville and Santa Cruz schools, and the staff at the Welfare Mothers' Support Network. This study would not have been possible without the cooperation of the families who graciously invited us into their homes and answered our questions.

ine low-income parents' goals and aspirations for their children and consider potential sources for the differences in the aspirations for children in middle childhood and those in adolescence. We pay special attention to how parents' experiences of poverty may affect their aspirations as well as their guidance, and we argue that the transition to adolescence may represent a key time, one at which parents and children reassess their goals and aspirations for the children's futures as well as the availability of resources that would enable the children to attain the goals.

Ecocultural Perspectives on Contexts of Development

Like others (for example, Bronfenbrenner, 1988; Harkness, Super, and Keefer, 1992; Lerner and Lerner, 1983; Rogoff, 1990; Whiting and Edwards, 1988), we have argued that to account for children's and adolescents' competence and vulnerability, social scientists need to move beyond describing stereotypical, global, and static features of culture toward developing multidimensional descriptions of the ecocultural niches of children and adolescents and their relationships. Our approach has been extensively informed by the ecocultural framework proposed by Tharp and Gallimore (1988) and Weisner, Gallimore, and Jordan (1988), which highlights ways that development and socialization occur in the activity settings of everyday life. The dimensions of family activity settings include *goals and values* of socialization; *scripts*, or patterns, of communication used to express universal human tasks of guidance, negotiation, planning, and conflict resolution; and key *personnel*, that is, the configurations of the primary relationships involved in socialization, including children's parents, siblings, extended kin, and fictive kin. Although these dimensions are interdependent, in this chapter we focus primarily on parents' goals and values and their guidance scripts for socializing their aspirations, and we consider how both developmental and societal factors associated with the transition from childhood to adolescence may lead to reassessments of both parents' and adolescents' goals and aspirations.

The ecocultural framework appears especially useful for investigating developmental stability and change within individuals, families, groups, and cultures (Cooper, in press; Goldenberg, Reese, Balzano, and Gallimore, 1993). Although not a formal theory of falsifiable propositions, the ecocultural framework dimensionalizes the qualities of individual, relational, and group change that allow researchers to test hypotheses in order to account for within-culture variation in both competence and vulnerability during childhood and adolescence. Thus, a key advantage of this multidimensional framework is that it avoids the stereotyping of cultural differences between mainstream and minority group children and adolescents in terms of deficits. Such stereotyping is a particular risk because so much research on U.S. minority youth has been driven by the problem orientation of criminal justice, drug, and adolescent pregnancy funding initiatives (Cooper, in press; McLoyd, 1989).

Role of Poverty in Parental Aspirations

Low-income parents from diverse ethnic groups have been described as holding low educational and vocational aspirations for their children, and such aspirations have been assumed to contribute to school failure, unemployment, and persistent poverty. Yet recent research portrays low-income parents as holding high aspirations for their children while differing in their abilities to guide their children toward achieving the parents' wishes (Heath, 1983; Reese, Balzano, Gallimore, and Goldenberg, 1991). However, Rodman and Voydanoff (1988) have shown that, although low-income parents hold high aspirations for their children, these parents also tend to express dreams and goals that are more modest. Rodman and Voydanoff suggest that such mitigation may reflect parents' accommodations to their limited resources and uncertain future.

This chapter specifically concerns the aspirations and guidance of low-income Mexican American and European American parents of children and adolescents. Mexican American families are experiencing severe unemployment and poverty, and school dropout rates of Mexican American youth are among the highest of minority students (Garcia, in press). In our program of research, in order to assess how dimensions of Mexican American culture may influence family socialization, we have focused on immigrant parents whose children were born in the United States. Many of these families immigrated to the United States so their children could get a good education that would allow them to move out of poverty; the immigrant parents themselves typically have only an elementary school education (Suarez-Orozco, 1991). Low-income European American families experience both persistent and temporary poverty for multiple reasons that include divorce, job loss, and life-style choice. They constitute the majority of those living in poverty in the United States but are often ignored in discussions of poverty, developmental risk, and school failure (McLoyd and Flanagan, 1990). Low-income European American parents' pessimism regarding education as a way out of their poverty has been proposed as an explanation for their children's poor performance in school (Heath, 1983), yet many questions remain concerning within-group differences in the aspirations and guidance of these families for their children.

Stability and Change in Aspirations and Guidance

Recent research is illuminating how stability and change in parental goals and aspirations occur differentially across domains. For example, in the People's Republic of China, Lee and Zhan (1991) found stability from the 1950s to 1980s in parents' moral values—particularly those rooted in the traditional Chinese culture—but not in the political values mandated by government leaders during the parents' own youth. Other studies suggest that parents' moral goals for their children may remain relatively unchanged while educational and vocational goals may be modified over time, either by feedback from children's interests, achievements, or difficulties (Goldenberg, Reese, Balzano, and Gallimore, 1993) or by the "cooling off" of parental expectations resulting from teachers' and counselors' gatekeeping (Erickson and Schultz, 1981). In this chapter, we explore stability and change in parents' educational, vocational, and personal/moral aspirations from middle childhood to early adolescence.

Contemporary discussions of stability and change in parental goals have been further enriched and sharpened by conceptions of hierarchies and timetables. The daily stresses of poverty may supersede parents' educational goals for children. For example, parents may place a higher priority on solving immediate financial problems than on long-term educational goals and may ask an older child to stay home to care for younger siblings or to seek employment to help the family rather than complete high school or a higher education. Similarly, parents may keep children home from school to protect them from neighborhood violence or such potential dangers at school as gang violence, drugs, or sexual activity. Thus, parents' aspirations for their child's or adolescent's personal safety, morality, or family obligations may supersede educational and vocational goals and lead to the parents' reassessing previously established goal hierarchies (Thomas, Chess, Sillen, and Mendez, 1974). Parental reassessments of goal hierarchies may also correspond to developmental timetables or watersheds, such as a child's transition from elementary into middle or junior high school. In addition to making vocational goals for a child more salient, issues associated with junior high school may affect the whole family (Eccles and others, 1993; Goodnow and Collins, 1990). For example, if adolescents fail exams, become pregnant, or drop out of school, then family goals and aspirations for the adolescents may be reevaluated and reconfigured in terms of the goals of other family members.

The Match-Mismatch Project

Our program of research explores linkages between family and school contexts of development during middle childhood and adolescence (see, for example, Azmitia and others, 1993; Cooper, Azmitia, and Garcia, 1993). As part of that exploration, we have been investigating the match-mismatch hypothesis, which posits that the educational failure of low-income students from diverse ethnic groups is due to mismatches between students' home and school cultures (Cazden, 1988; Heath, 1983). Proposed sources of family-school mismatches include discrepancies in goals and aspirations and in scripts, including guidance and learning patterns. More broadly, this hypothesis reflects the view that developmental competencies and vulnerabilities can be explained by the goodness of fit between the family or child and cultural contexts and institutions (Eccles and others, 1993; Thomas, Chess, Sillen, and Mendez, 1974). Early discussions of the match-mismatch and the goodness-of-fit hypotheses tended to ignore variability within cultural groups and, especially in the case of the match-mismatch hypothesis, to pay little attention to potential developmental shifts in sources of competence and vulnerability. The approach we take in this chapter is consistent with the more recent formulations of these two hypotheses, which take into account between-group as well as within-group variability (for example, Eccles and others, 1993; Schmitt-Rodermund and Silbereisen, 1993).

As part of our study, we asked low-income Mexican American and European American parents of third-, fifth-, and seventh-grade children to describe their own educational, vocational, and personal/moral aspirations for their children and to say how they were helping their children attain these aspirations. In an earlier study (Azmitia, Cooper, and Garcia, 1993), we mapped parents' aspirations across the educational, vocational, and personal/moral domains and showed how their perceptions of their own expertise in a domain influenced their strategies for helping their children attain these aspirations. In what follows, we briefly summarize these domain-related patterns and then examine differences in parental aspirations and guidance in relation to children's ages, paying special attention to the transition between middle childhood and adolescence. Differences in parents' strategies related to children's ages may be influenced by parental theories about child and adolescent development (Goodnow and Collins, 1990). For example, Smetana (1988) has documented a shift in the amount of responsibility parents give to adolescents in decisions about their educational and vocational future. Here, we explore whether such a shift is evident among low-income families who are accommodating to a new culture or to a poverty niche.

Another goal of our research was to explore variability in parents' aspirations and guidance patterns within Mexican American and European American groups, as well as examining similarities and differences between them, since relying solely on comparisons between groups may foster misperceptions that one is deficient relative to the other (McLoyd, 1991). In our earlier study (Azmitia, Cooper, and Garcia, 1993), we reported quantitative analyses of our data. In this chapter, we describe qualitative features of our data that illuminate developmental processes that may be involved in the reassessment and renegotiation of parents' aspirations for their children's educational, vocational, and personal/moral development during middle childhood and adolescence. Finally, to explore potential hierarchies among goals, we also examine child age–related patterns in aspirations and guidance across domains.

Research Participants, Procedures, and Measures

Our data are drawn from responses from a sample of seventy-two low-income families (thirty-six Mexican American and thirty-six European American) with children in the third, fifth, and seventh grades. In each age group of each ethnic group, the children were evenly divided among boys and girls; thus, we interviewed the families of six boys and of six girls for each age/ethnic group. Families were considered low-income if their children were receiving free or reduced-price school lunches. They were recruited through elementary and junior high schools and from referrals from other participants in the study, and each family was paid $25.00 for its participation. All the families lived in two small neighboring cities in central California, one an agricultural community (population approximately 30,000), and the other a small coastal city (population approximately 50,000). Because ecocultural theory calls for an analysis of the history and social context in which families are embedded (Tharp and Gallimore, 1988), we supplement the typical demographic information that follows with material about the families' history and social context, particularly as it reveals the etiology of their poverty.

Eighty-three percent of the Mexican American families were headed by two parents. One participating child was an only child; the rest had between one and ten siblings (mean = 3.19). In twelve Mexican American families, other relatives (typically parents' siblings) lived in the home. Eighty-six percent of the fathers and 74 percent of the mothers were employed, typically as farm laborers or in canneries. Most were concerned because area canneries and food processing plants were then closing and moving to Mexico. Most parents described themselves as literate in Spanish but not in English and had not gone beyond elementary school (mode for fathers was third grade; for mothers, sixth grade). The poverty of these Mexican American families appeared to be long standing. For example, many had lived for several years in trailers or labor camps, and their homes were generally small and sparsely furnished. Many parents spontaneously expressed concern about the presence of drug dealers and gang violence in their neighborhoods; several had invested in Nintendo games to keep their children indoors. They also reported they could not afford many recreational activities but enjoyed visiting relatives and attending the local flea market.

Eighty-one percent of the European American families were headed by a single parent, in all but two cases, the mother. Six participating children were only children; the rest had between one and four siblings (mean = 1.69). Eleven European American families had other adults, typically housemates or partners, living in the home. Parents reported that 81 percent of the fathers and 33 percent of the mothers were employed; the primary employment categories were skilled manual worker, craftsperson, clerical or sales worker, and menial houseworker. All European American parents reported that they were literate in English; most had completed high school, and many had some junior college experience. From all indications, for 81 percent ($N = 29$) of the European American families the onset of poverty was recent, typically the result of divorce. These families lived in middle-class or working-class neighborhoods and remarked that they frequently had to remind their children that they could no longer afford many amenities. Many indicated that except for traffic, their neighborhoods were relatively safe. The remaining 19 percent of the families ($N = 7$) appeared to have been experiencing pervasive poverty; five of these families had been long-time residents in a neighborhood known for affordable rents but made dangerous by drug traffickers, prostitutes, and gangs, and two families indicated they been homeless several times over the past few years. Like the Mexican American parents, this latter group of European American parents reported that they tried to keep their children inside to protect them from the dangers of drug trafficking and being approached by strangers.

All parents were interviewed in their homes, in separate rooms whenever possible if there were two parents. If only one parent was available, one interviewer asked the questions while the other recorded the parent's responses. One Mexican American parent preferred to be interviewed in English, but all the rest of the Mexican American parents were interviewed in Spanish by a team of native Spanish speakers, including three of the authors. Each interview lasted about one hour and was recorded on audiotape.

The interview, developed for the purpose of the study, was piloted on a sample of low-income European American parents with children in the third, fifth, and seventh grades. The Spanish version was developed and piloted by Mexican-born staff members from low-income backgrounds, one of whom worked as a translator. The interview covered demographic information about household members and included questions regarding personnel involved in chores and homework activity settings; instructional scripts for those settings; and parents' long-term aspirations for and guidance of their child's educational, occupational, and personal maturity. Only the parents' long-term aspirations and strategies for helping their children attain these goals are addressed in this chapter. Parents were asked open-ended questions about these long-term aspirations. For each type of aspiration, parents were first asked about their goals: for example, How much education do you want your child to complete? What job or profession would you like your child to attain? What type of person [for example, qualities, values] would you like your child to be when he or she grows up? Then parents were asked how they were helping their child attain these aspirations.

Interview Results

In this section, we first review and illustrate our findings regarding overall similarities and differences between Mexican American and European American parents' aspirations and guidance, and then we examine differences within each group of families. In general, the data support our hypothesis that, at least in educational and vocational domains, parents' aspirations and guidance patterns appear to differ according to whether the child is in middle childhood or adolescence. However, aspirations and guidance patterns appear stable across age groups in the moral domain, perhaps reflecting parents' expertise within that domain (Azmitia and others, 1993), their hierarchy of goals, or their response to a poverty niche in which there is greater potential for straying away from the good path or *buen camino*.

Between-Group Patterns Across Domains. Our findings about educational aspirations were consistent with those of Reese, Balzano, Gallimore, and Goldenberg (1991): both the Mexican American and European American groups of parents held high educational aspirations for their children. As one Mexican American parent said, "We aren't here [in the United States] because we like working here or like to live here. . . . We live better in Mexico. But I make this sacrifice because I want them to study, to learn English." However, more of the Mexican American parents indicated that they would be content for their children to finish high school, whereas more of the European American parents expressed hopes that their children would attend graduate school, although these parents were also more likely to allow the child to choose his or her ultimate level of education. As one European American parent stated, "I don't want to impose anything on him, but I do tell him he has to study. I don't tell him he has to study such and such because I like it. . . . I just want him to study a short [attainable] career so that he has a future." Mexican American parents were more likely than European American parents to report using indirect strategies, such as providing encouragement or support, using their own lives as examples of the costs of a poor education, or enlisting the help of siblings and relatives to help children attain their aspirations; whereas European American parents were more likely to report using direct strategies, such as providing tutoring or advice on course selection and study skills. It is likely that the Mexican American and European American parents' aspirations and guidance strategies reflect the parents' own educational differences. For parents with little schooling, finishing high school may represent a great achievement, but those with college experience may have higher expectations. Also, by the time they had reached fifth grade, many Mexican American children had exceeded their parents' schooling, and thus, many parents had to rely on more indirect guidance strategies.

As in other studies (for example, Matute-Bianchi and Alvarez, 1990), Mexican American parents in our sample held high occupational aspirations for their children; many hoped their children would become doctors, lawyers, or teachers. European American parents in the sample typically reported that their occupational aspirations would be the choices of their children. Although parents in both groups saw themselves helping their children attain their occupational aspirations by offering encouragement, help, advice, and tutoring, there were some differences. Mexican American parents again were more likely to mention using themselves as negative role models, telling their children not to work as farm laborers or in the cannery. One parent remarked that "anything" was acceptable "as long as it isn't in the fields. . . . When I was very young, I started to pick strawberries, and I wouldn't want him to do that." Although European American parents also used their lives as models for their children, the tone of their examples was more positive. For example, many told their children that despite making mistakes, such as dropping out of school or getting married too young, they were now attempting to correct these mistakes (for example, they had gotten their high school equivalency degrees and were enrolled in community college), so they could get the training needed for their own vocational aspiration. Many also remarked that their good study habits served as a model for their children.

However, we also saw potential vulnerabilities in low-income parents' educational and vocational aspirations. Like Reese, Balzano, Gallimore, and

Goldenberg (1991), for example, we found that even though low-income parents held high occupational aspirations for their children, some did not know that their children's vocational goals required a college education, while others who did seek college educations for their children were unsure about application and financial aid procedures. Other vulnerabilities were indicated by the fear or ambivalence towards school expressed by some Mexican American and European American parents in our sample, particularly parents of adolescents. Many Mexican American parents held hopes for education as a way out of poverty and wanted their children to be successful yet also expressed concerns about the hazards of drugs, sex, and violence in junior high school or concerns about children's advanced education making the children distant from their families and communities. Said one parent, "I have seen other people—that their children spend years in school, and for what? All they learn are vices, and in the end, they no longer feel comfortable in our community and then they aren't comfortable anywhere, at home or at school." In contrast, European American parents expressed high aspirations, but some were skeptical that schools could help their children acquire skills needed to succeed while others worried whether they had the financial or emotional resources to guide their children towards maturity. One parent advised, "See if they want to go to college, 'cause you never know if one of them wants to do a trade. . . . If [my child] can stay out of trouble, he may want to be a mechanic." Some recently divorced parents also mentioned that they were more preoccupied with such immediate concerns as paying the rent, completing homework, or dealing with their children's misbehavior than with the children's long-term vocational and educational future.

Parents in both Mexican American and European American groups had personal and moral aspirations for their children and expressed hopes that their children would be moral persons, respect others and themselves, and stay away from drugs, gangs, and other "vices." As detailed in Azmitia and others (1993), parents in both groups provided tutoring and advice in this domain in which they saw themselves as experts, often using their own lives as positive examples of values they hoped their children would exhibit in adulthood. Said a European American parent, "I am helping her by being who I am as a mother, . . . also by learning for myself to love and to serve people. I talk to her a lot, and I am honest with me about what is happening in my life." Especially striking was parents' determination to keep children on the good path, the *buen camino* (Reese, Balzano, Gallimore, and Goldenberg, 1991). As one Mexican American parent said, "Right now [my child] is a very serious and good girl. I try that she is always busy so she does not go out and hang around [and pick up vices]. I want things to stay this way until she is grown up." Similarly, a European American parent said, "I try to talk to [my daughter], you know, about things that I see in the world that I don't like, that I wouldn't like a kid to do, I talk to [her] about it."

Like the work of Reese, Balzano, Gallimore, and Goldenberg (1991), our study illustrated the substantial moral capital that low-income parents have available to help children attain the parents' personal and moral aspirations. The lack of variability in these aspirations and guidance patterns suggests that moral values occupy a high priority in parents' hierarchy of goals. For many parents, the forces that can lead children away from the good path lie outside the home in the neighborhood or the school, and protecting children from these dangers takes precedence over other goals. The threat to which these parents were trying to respond is illustrated by the fact that during the course of our study, several drive-by shootings occurred in the low-income communities, and the older sister of one of our participating children was assaulted and killed in a schoolyard.

Age-Related Patterns Among Mexican American Families. Interviews of Mexican American parents of third graders revealed that the salient parental educational and vocational goals for these children derived from the parents' hopes that an education and career were a way out of poverty. The most salient moral goal was respect for others, especially elders, and for oneself. Parents reported helping their children attain these aspirations by telling them to stay in school and out of trouble and by giving moral lessons about what would happen if they did not, using the parents themselves and others as examples. For example, one parent recalled that "once [when] it was . . . 4:30, so the men were [still] in the fields picking artichokes, . . . I said, 'You see *mijo* [my son], that's a tough job, day after day until the sun goes down they have to be out there if it's hot or cold. Yes, *mijo*, that is why you guys need an education, because if you guys don't get enough education, you won't qualify for another job, and you will be doing that for a living.' . . . I don't know if at his age it will stick, but hopefully it will."

Despite the undercurrent of hope and dreams running through parents' educational and vocational aspirations, like Goldenberg, Reese, Balzano, and Gallimore (1993), we found that a few parents had adjusted their aspirations, based on feedback about their children's school performance or on a realistic assessment of their own ability to help their children achieve educational and vocational goals. For example, three parents said they hoped their children would become doctors or lawyers, but then added that they did not know if that was really possible. One said, for example, "I'd like him to be a lawyer. . . . Well, really, that is the dream that one has, that one's children succeed, that they are, how can I say it, better. That they do the things one was not able to do. . . . We say, 'We hope this boy continues studying and has a small career.' Not a doctor or a lawyer, because who knows?"

Mexican American parents of fifth graders also emphasized staying in school, but some indicated both ambivalence about their educational goals and despair as to how they might help their children achieve them. These parents were also less likely to mention professional occupations for children of this age, and if they did describe such aspirations, they might indicate that they would also be content with their children's becoming secretaries, mechanics, or store clerks. Finally, some parents indicated that, by fifth grade, children should take some responsibility for achieving goals and aspirations, saying for example,

"Well, I have the dream that he be somebody, but he still needs to put his share into this." The difference connected with age was especially evident in the domains of educational and occupational aspirations. The key age-related difference in the moral domain among Mexican American parents appeared in guidance strategies; parents of fifth graders mentioned that they gave explanations of issues and engaged their children in discussions about those issues, whereas parents of third graders were more likely to use more unilateral strategies, such as directives, praise, and punishment, to guide their children.

In educational and vocational domains, Mexican American parents of seventh graders tended to express lower aspirations than parents of third and fifth graders. Only a few mentioned college as a possibility for their children, and for some, even high school was in doubt. The theme that children should forge their own dreams and choose their own occupations was even more marked, suggesting that these parents may expect their adolescents to take responsibility for developing an educational and occupational identity. Many parents now simply said that as long as their children did not end up working in the fields or the cannery, any job would be fine. Unlike parents of younger children, parents of seventh graders did not disclose much planning or detail as to how they were helping their children attain their vocational goals; perhaps this finding is another indication of a shift in the jurisdiction of responsibility for achievement. One parent said, "I would like [my daughter] to get to college, . . . but the way things are now, who knows?" Another, when asked what job she wanted for her daughter, said, "Well, not a job like mine [field worker]—that she works in a store or something that is not so heavy." When the interviewer asked what this parent was doing to help her daughter achieve that goal, the parent asked, "What do you mean?" And when the interviewer then asked if the parent had made any plans to help her daughter end up working in a store, the answer was no. However, this lack of planning may also reflect the lack of fit between parents' and children's competencies (Eccles and others, 1993); parents with an elementary school education may feel unqualified to plan their adolescents' vocational and educational futures, particularly when these parents find themselves in a new culture with unfamiliar schools and occupations.

Although our finding that Mexican American parents of adolescents held lower vocational and educational aspirations than Mexican American parents of elementary school children parallels findings of Reese, Balzano, Gallimore, and Goldenberg's longitudinal study (1991), the cross-sectional design of our study does not allow us to determine whether these lower expectations of parents of seventh graders represent an age-related shift. Because our study concerned immigrant families, the pattern of lower expectations could reflect a cohort effect; for example, the older children may have been less fluent in English or may have had more responsibilities for work and child care than younger children, and such differences could have affected their schooling. We are currently examining the school achievement data of participating children to determine whether the adolescents were doing more poorly in school than the elementary school-aged children. If so, their poorer performance may have contributed to their parents' lower educational and vocational aspirations for them.

In contrast to age-related differences in educational and occupational domains, in the moral domain, parents of adolescents resembled those of younger children in emphasizing having respect and being honest, responsible, and a good person despite being poor, and in providing modeling and direct guidance. Said one parent, "We are people who are very poor, but we don't give [our children] bad examples about anything. We behave well, hoping that they will learn to behave. If they see that we behave and are good persons, hopefully they will do the same."

Age-Related Patterns Among European American Families. European American parents of third graders expressed a wide range of educational and vocational aspirations, but their moral aspirations were consistently high, with respect for self and others being valued most highly. Like Mexican American parents, some European American parents had devoted much effort to planning their children's futures, yet others indicated that they had not given much thought to such planning but were concentrating on helping their children attain personal and moral aspirations. As one parent remarked: "I haven't thought about it too much. Education is not a big priority. It is more important that kids be emotionally healthy and happy. . . . I'm looking at the possibilities [for educational and vocational goals] and helping them learn to choose for themselves." Even parents who expressed high aspirations tended to express reservations or add more modest goals also, conveying the view that control over the future was beyond their or their children's control, a finding consistent with the work of Rodman and Voydanoff (1988).

European American parents of fifth graders also expressed a wide range of aspirations. Like European American parents of third graders, they viewed educational and occupational aspirations as their children's choice, but unlike the parents of third graders, some expressed doubts about their own ability to guide their children to maturity. Notably, they did not link education to vocational aspirations but rather linked both educational and vocational domains to moral goals, perhaps because of the value they placed on moral and personal development or perhaps because of their own personal struggles. For example, one parent said, "I'm not one who dreams about my child's future. I still feel lost in trying to find my future. But I hope that he'll value education. And that he'll become educated just because . . . that's what you need in life, whether it applies to your job or not." Parents of fifth graders also were unlike parents of third graders in the concern they expressed about the adequacy of their children's schooling, particularly its ability to teach skills the children needed to succeed in the broader world. As one parent said, "We're real . . . pro-school, pro-family. We try and let [our child] know this is the way our society works, you go to school for so many years. . . . I don't think that's where learning takes place particularly . . . [but] I don't voice this negativity to him."

Despite the concerns and doubts expressed by some European American parents, others expressed confidence in guiding their fifth-graders towards the future, at least in general terms. Said one mother, "I would like her to complete high school, and at least four years of college. . . . When I grew up a high school diploma was a real important thing. Now, in this day and age, a high school diploma doesn't mean beans. You've gotta have college. . . . The fact that I went back to school is a big help for her. [I] also take her going on some cleaning jobs with me [the mother cleaned houses for a living] and actually knowing how hard it is— . . . I told her the more education you get, the more money you get and the easier the job is."

Like European American parents of younger children, European American parents of seventh graders held high aspirations for their children's moral and personal development and were consistently concerned about their children's safety and their staying on the good path. Many saw education as a way to enhance children's safety, protecting them from drugs and from becoming prostitutes, and some parents took their children to the parents' Alcoholics Anonymous meetings. Although there were exceptions, most parents of seventh graders, in contrast to parents of younger children, were active in helping their children attain their educational and vocational goals. This engagement appeared to have been triggered by the young adolescents' formulating initial vocational interests to which parents could respond by finding opportunities for the adolescents to explore and develop these interests. For example, one parent reported purchasing anatomy coloring books for a daughter who was interested in a medical career, and another mentioned finding volunteer opportunities at the local SPCA for a son aspiring to be a veterinarian. It is notable that the vocational experiences sought were not arranged within the school. Unlike the low-income families in Heath's study (1983), these parents were not questioning the value of education but rather the quality of the schools. The parents who expressed such doubts may have been those who moved into conditions of poverty and enrolled their child in a school in a lower-income neighborhood the most recently. This pattern of parental involvement may also reflect parents' views of occupational identity as primarily a task of adolescence and young adulthood (Goodnow and Collins, 1990).

Conclusions

Our findings supported our hypothesis that the role of parental goals for children and of the linkages from family to community contexts of development differs between the children's middle childhood and adolescence. However, this age-related difference was evident only in vocational and educational domains. Across the age span we studied, parents' moral aspirations and level of involvement remained uniformly high, although their mode of involvement shifted in ways reflecting their children's growing developmental competencies.

In the Mexican American group, parents of fifth and seventh graders held lower educational and vocational aspirations than those of third graders. They also were more likely to view academic and vocational success as partly their children's responsibility. This pattern may reflect parents' developmental timetables for children or that many children in the fifth grade had exceeded their parents' schooling and parents felt unable to help them. In the European American group, the major age-related difference occurred between elementary school (third and fifth grade) and adolescence (seventh grade). Unlike parents of third and fifth graders, parents of seventh graders were actively involved in guiding their children's educational and vocational aspirations, a pattern that may have been triggered by young adolescents' formulating their educational and vocational interests.

In this chapter, we have focused on parents' aspirations and strategies for guiding children towards maturity, but both groups of parents also saw their children's roles as crucial, especially in the children's educational and vocational development, as seen in parents' transferring responsibility for these two domains to children as early as fifth grade. In contrast, parents' continued involvement in children's personal and moral guidance suggests that they viewed responsibility over the moral domain as either too important to be delegated or as a prerogative that their expertise enabled them to retain.

In our current work, we are interviewing children and adolescents to assess their goals and aspirations and to determine how they are integrating the different goals and contexts of their lives. The complexity of developing an adaptive coordination across developmental contexts is reflected by the accounts of Phelan, Davidson, and Cao (1991) of the struggles of high school students to integrate their views of themselves with their experiences across the multiple worlds of family, school, and peer relationships. Our study suggests that an important issue is parents' maintaining their high aspirations for their children's educational and vocational attainment from the early elementary school years through adolescence. Because our work was cross-sectional, we cannot draw definitive conclusions about what factors contributed to the age-related differences we found in parents' vocational and educational aspirations. For example, as we mentioned earlier, patterns for the Mexican American group may have been influenced by cohort effects. Nevertheless, it is likely that children's school performance provides parents with feedback about the likelihood that their children will attain parental aspirations (Goldenberg, Reese, Balzano, and Gallimore, 1993). However, because academic gatekeeping begins in the late middle childhood and early adolescent years (Henderson and Dweck, 1990), it will be important to determine if parents are receiving accurate feedback about their children's progress. Parental aspirations may also decline as children exceed the parents' educational level and the parents can no longer offer guidance or must confront the costs of a college education. We are pursuing these longitudinal questions in a study of the transition from middle childhood to adolescence in a sample of low-income Mexican American and European American fifth graders. In another project (Cooper, Jackson, Azmitia, and Lopez, 1993), we are investigating how participation in academic outreach programs can keep students in the academic pipeline toward college and vocational success. In this research, African American and Latino adolescents have described adult mentors and peers in their academic outreach programs as sources of both emotional and instrumental support in bridging what can be a bewildering array of goals and expectations across the multiple worlds described by Phelan, Davidson, and Cao (1991).

Overall, the findings we have discussed regarding stability and change in parents' goals and guidance patterns demonstrate how ecocultural analyses of activity settings can help researchers unbundle global or stereotypical characterizations of diverse cultural groups and point to important sources of within-group as well as between-group variability. We do not claim that our samples are representative of all Mexican Americans or European Americans living in poverty, but rather than pursue mythical representative samples, we consider it more useful to provide ballpark descriptions of parameters of samples linked to key ecocultural dimensions, such as communities of origin, generation and goals of immigration, family structure, and languages spoken (Schofield and Anderson, 1986). Finally, we continue to be struck by the variability within each ethnic or social class group we have studied, and we are exploring such within-group variability more systematically, in hopes of identifying sources of both competence and vulnerability in the linkages of the multiple worlds of children and adolescents.

References

Azmitia, M., Cooper, C. R., and Garcia, E. E. "Mentoring for Maturity: Guidance of Children and Adolescents by Low-Income Mexican American and European American Families." Unpublished study, University of California at Santa Cruz, 1993.

Azmitia, M., Cooper, C. R., Garcia, E. E., Rivera, L., and Martínez-Chávez, R. "Within-Group and Within-Family Variability in Mexican American Children and Adolescents' Educational Achievement." Paper presented at the meeting of the American Educational Research Association, Atlanta, Ga., Aug. 1993.

Bronfenbrenner, U. "Foreword." In A. R. Pence (ed.), *Ecological Research with Children and Families: From Concepts to Methodology*. New York: Teachers College Press, 1988.

Cazden, C. B. *Classroom Discourse*. Portsmouth, N.H.: Heinemann Educational Books, 1988.

Cooper, C. R. "Cultural Perspectives on Continuity and Change Across the Contexts of Adolescents' Relationships." In R. Montemayor, G. R. Adams, and T. Gullotta (eds.), *Advances in Adolescent Development*, Vol. 6: *Personal Relationships During Adolescence*. Newbury Park, Calif.: Sage, in press.

Cooper, C. R., Azmitia, M., and Garcia, E. E. "Matches and Mismatches Between Family and School Cultures: Consequences for Children and Adolescents from Culturally and Linguistically Diverse Families." Paper presented at the meeting of the American Educational Research Association, Atlanta, Apr. 1993.

Cooper, C. R., Jackson, J. F., Azmitia, M., and Lopez, E. M. "Multiple Selves, Multiple Worlds: Ethnically Sensitive Research on Identity, Relationships, and Opportunity Structures in Adolescence." In V. McLoyd and L. Steinberg (eds.), *Conceptual and Methodological Issues in the Study of Minority Adolescents and Their Families*. Unpublished manuscript, 1993.

Eccles, J. S., Midgley, C., Wigfield, A., Buchanan, C. M., Reuman, D., Flanagan, C., and MacIver, D. "Development During Adolescence: The Impact of Stage-Environment Fit on Young Adolescents' Experiences in Schools and in Families." *American Psychologist*, 1993, *48*, 90–101.

Erickson, F., and Shultz, J. *The Counselor as Gatekeeper: Social Interaction in Interviews.* San Diego, Calif.: Academic Press, 1981.

Garcia, E. E. "'Hispanic' Children: Theoretical, Empirical, and Related Policy Issues." *Educational Psychology Review,* in press.

Goldenberg, C., Reese, L., Balzano, S., and Gallimore, R. "Cause or Effect? Latino Children's School Performance and Their Parents' Educational Expectations." Paper presented at the meeting of the American Educational Research Association, Atlanta, Apr. 1993.

Goodnow, J. J., and Collins, W. A. *Development According to Parents: The Nature, Sources, and Consequences of Parents' Ideas.* Hillsdale, N.J.: Erlbaum, 1990.

Harkness, S., Super, C. M., and Keefer, C. M. "Learning to Be an American Parent: How Cultural Models Give Directive Force." In R. D'Andrade and C. Strauss (eds.), *Human Motives and Cultural Models.* New York: Cambridge University Press, 1992.

Heath, S. B. *Ways with Words.* New York: Cambridge University Press, 1983.

Henderson, V. L., and Dweck, C. S. "Motivation and Achievement." In S. S. Feldman and G. R. Elliot (eds.), *At the Threshold: The Developing Adolescent.* Cambridge, Mass.: Harvard University Press, 1990.

Lee, L. C., and Zhan, G. Q. "Political Socialization and Parental Values in the People's Republic of China." *International Journal of Behavioral Development,* 1991, *14,* 337–373.

Lerner, J. V., and Lerner, R. M. "Temperament and Adaptation Across Life: Theoretical and Empirical Issues." In P. B. Baltes and O. G. Brim, Jr. (eds.), *Life-Span Development and Behavior.* Vol. 5. San Diego, Calif.: Academic Press, 1983.

McLoyd, V. C. "Socialization and Development in a Changing Economy: The Effects of Paternal Job and Income Loss on Children." *American Psychologist,* 1989, *44,* 393–402.

McLoyd, V. C. "What Is the Study of African American Children the Study of?" In R. J. Jones (ed.), *Black Psychology.* (3rd ed.) Berkeley, Calif.: Cobb and Henry, 1991.

McLoyd, V. C., and Flanagan, C. A. "Economic Stress: Effects on Family Life and Child Development." *New Directions for Child Development,* no. 46. San Francisco: Jossey-Bass, 1990.

Matute-Bianchi, M. E., and Alvarez, L. P. "Analysis of Project Theme Ethnographic Data." In M. McClaren-Lightly (ed)., *Research for the 1990s: Proceedings of the Linguistic Minority Research Project.* Santa Cruz: University of California, Santa Cruz, 1990.

Mehan, H. "Understanding Inequality in Schools: The Contribution of Interpretive Studies." *Sociology of Education,* 1992, *65,* 1–20.

Moll, L. C., Velez-Ibanez, C., and Gonzalez, N. "Funds of Knowledge." Santa Cruz: National Center for Research on Cultural Diversity and Second Language Learning, University of California, Santa Cruz, 1991.

Phelan, P., Davidson, A. L., and Cao, H. T. "Students' Multiple Worlds: Negotiating the Boundaries of Family, Peer, and School Cultures." *Anthropology and Education Quarterly,* 1991, *22,* 224–250.

Reese, L., Balzano, S., Gallimore, R., and Goldenberg, C. "The Concept of Educación: Latino Family Values and American Schooling." Paper presented at the meeting of the American Anthropological Association, Chicago, Apr. 1991.

Rodman, H., and Voydanoff, P. "Social Class and Parents' Range of Aspirations for Their Children." *Journal of Social Issues,* 1988, *23,* 333–344.

Rogoff, B. *Apprenticeship in Thinking: Cognitive Development in Social Context.* New York: Oxford University Press, 1990.

Schmitt-Rodermund, E., and Silbereisen, R. K. "Adolescents' Age Expectations and Adjustment During Acculturation of German Families from Eastern Europe." Paper presented at the meeting of the Society for Research in Child Development, New Orleans, Mar. 1993.

Schofield, J. W., and Anderson, K. "Combining Quantitative and Qualitative Components of Research on Ethnic Identity and Intergroup Relations." In J. S. Phinney and M. J. Rotheram (eds.), *Children's Ethnic Socialization: Pluralism and Development.* Newbury Park, Calif.: Sage, 1986.

Smetana, J. G. "Adolescents' and Parents' Conceptions of Parental Authority." *Child Development*, 1988, *59*, 321–335.

Suarez-Orozco, M. M. "Immigrant Adaptation to Schooling: A Hispanic Case." In M. A. Gibson and J. U. Ogbu (eds.), *Minority Status and Schooling*. New York: Garland, 1991.

Tharp, R. G., and Gallimore, R. *Rousing Minds to Life: Teaching, Learning, and Schooling in Social Context*. New York: Cambridge University Press, 1988.

Thomas, A., Chess, S., Sillen, J., and Mendez, O. "Cross-cultural Study of Behavior in Children with Special Vulnerabilities to Stress." In M. Roff and D. F. Ricks (eds.), *Life History Research in Psychopathology*. Minneapolis: University of Minnesota Press, 1974.

Weisner, T. S., Gallimore, R., and Jordan, C. "Unpackaging Cultural Effects on Classroom Learning: Native Hawaiian Peer Assistance and Child-Generated Activity." *Anthropology and Education Quarterly*, 1988, *19*, 327–351.

Whiting, B. B., and Edwards, C. P. *Children of Different Worlds*. Cambridge, Mass.: Harvard University Press, 1988.

CATHERINE R. COOPER is professor of psychology and education at the University of California, Santa Cruz.

MARGARITA AZMITIA is associate professor of psychology at the University of California, Santa Cruz.

EUGENE E. GARCIA is professor of education and psychology at the University of California, Santa Cruz.

ANGELA ITTEL is a doctoral student in developmental psychology at the University of California, Santa Cruz.

EDWARD LOPEZ is a doctoral student in developmental psychology at the University of California, Santa Cruz.

LOURDES RIVERA is a graduate student in education at the University of California, Santa Cruz.

REBECA MARTÍNEZ-CHÁVEZ is a research associate in the Center for Research in Cultural Diversity and Second Language Learning at the University of California, Santa Cruz.

INDEX

Activities, program, 25; features of successful, 60–61; project-based, 52–53, 54, 56, 59–61; required variety in, 44; school age child care, 13–14; as work, 30–31

Adolescents: contact with adults, 6, 25, 28–29, 31, 32, 78–79; contemporary socialization of, 5–6; hazards facing, 70–71, 73, 77; learning valued by, 31–34; parental aspirations for, 75–79

Adults: adolescent contact with, 6, 25, 28–29, 31, 32, 78–79; children teaching and learning with, 39–40, 47, 48; as evaluators, 30. *See also* Parental aspirations for children

African American children, 41, 48

After-school programs: activities in, 13–14, 18–19, 20; computer-oriented, 7, 35–36; materials design for, 19–20, 62–63; theories on, 14, 21, 36–41, 53. *See also* School age child care programs

Age of students, parental aspirations and, 74–78

Alone at home, children, 6, 16–17

Alvarez, L. P., 72

Anderson, K., 79

Armstrong, T., 14

Arts and crafts activities, 17–18

Ascher, C., 7, 23

Aspirations. *See* Parental aspirations for children

Assessment, program: performance-related, 7, 45–46; skills and knowledge, 46–48

Attendance: program, 58; school, 32, 72, 74, 77

Azmitia, M., 68, 69, 71, 73, 78, 81

Baltes, P. B., 3, 4

Balzano, S., 66, 67–68, 71, 72–73, 74, 78

Benson, P. L., 6

Bernard, B., 6, 8

Bilingual communication, 40–41; Spanish-English, 38, 47–48

Blumenfeld, P., 53

Boston, 52

Bronfenbrenner, U., 3, 4

Brown, J. S., 53

Brustel Corporation, 17, 21

Bulletin board, children's computer, 38

California, 41, 42, 47–48, 69–70

Cao, H. T., 78, 79

Carnegie Council on Adolescent Development, 4, 5, 6, 25, 41

Case study skills measurement, 47

Cazden, C. B., 68

Center for the Study of Social Policy, 5, 6

Change, developmental stability and, 66, 67–68

Chard, S., 53

Chess, S., 68

Child care programs. *See* School age child care programs

Children's Defense Fund, 4

Children's Television Workshop (CTW), 7, 11–22; science and math kits, 15, 17–20

Clark, R. M., 8

Cole, M., 36, 46, 49

Collins, A., 21, 52, 53

Collins, W. A., 68, 69, 77

Comer, J. P., 4

Community-based programs: independent, 26–29, 40–41; university settings for, 42–43, 49

Computer literacy, 36, 38–41; testing, 47

Contexts for learning, 4–5; adaptive coordination across, 78–79; computer-oriented, 36, 38–41, 47; contemporary youth socialization and, 5–6; critical factors affecting, 62–63, 78–79; ecocultural perspectives on, 66, 79; family, 66; family-school mismatches as, 68–69; inner-city organizations as, 31–34; multisite program, 35–36, 48–49; safety of, 26, 29, 31, 70–71, 73, 74, 77

Control groups, wait-list, 44–45

Cooper, C. R., 7, 66, 68, 69, 71, 73, 78, 81

Cooperation, learning, 18–19

Cremin, L., 53

Crouter, A. C., 3

CTW. *See* Children's Television Workshop

Ordering Information

New Directions for Child Development is a series of paperback books that presents the latest research findings on all aspects of children's psychological development, including their cognitive, social, moral, and emotional growth. Books in the series are published quarterly in Fall, Winter, Spring, and Summer and are available for purchase by subscription and individually.

Subscriptions for 1994 cost $54.00 for individuals (a savings of 25 percent over single-copy prices) and $75.00 for institutions, agencies, and libraries. Please do not send institutional checks for personal subscriptions. Standing orders are accepted.

Single copies cost $17.95 when payment accompanies order. (California, New Jersey, New York, and Washington, D.C., residents please include appropriate sales tax.) All orders will be charged postage and handling.

Discounts for quantity orders are available. Please write to the address below for information.

All orders must include either the name of an individual or an official purchase order number. Please submit your order as follows:
   Subscriptions: specify series and year subscription is to begin
   Single copies: include individual title code (such as CD59)

Mail all orders to:
   Jossey-Bass Publishers
   350 Sansome Street
   San Francisco, California 94104-1342

For single-copy sales outside of the United States, contact:
   Maxwell Macmillan International Publishing Group
   866 Third Avenue
   New York, New York 10022-6221

For subscription sales outside of the United States, contact any international subscription agency or Jossey-Bass directly.

OTHER TITLES AVAILABLE IN THE
NEW DIRECTIONS FOR CHILD DEVELOPMENT SERIES
William Damon, Editor-in-Chief